MW00653175

Tales of
Potential

Tales of Potential

THE CINDERELLA STORY YOU HAVEN'T HEARD

Joanna Bloor

THE AMPLIFY LAB
OAKLAND, CALIFORNIA

Copyright © 2023 by Joanna Bloor

All rights reserved. No part of this publication may be reproduced, distributed or transmitted in any form or by any means, including photocopying, recording, or other electronic or mechanical methods, without the prior written permission of the publisher, except in the case of brief quotations embodied in critical reviews and certain other noncommercial uses permitted by copyright law. For permission requests, write to the publisher, addressed "Attention: Permissions Coordinator," at the address below.

Joanna Bloor/Amplify Lab
info@joannabloor.com

Ordering Information: Quantity sales. Special discounts are available on quantity purchases by corporations, associations, and others. For details, contact the "Special Sales Department" at the email address above.

Tales of Potential: The Cinderella Story You Haven't Heard/ Joanna Bloor. — 1st ed.
ISBN: 979-8-9862226-1-5, paperback
ISBN: 979-8-9862226-2-2, ebook
ISBN: 979-8-9862226-3-9, hardcover

Illustrations by Raisa Effress
Book design by HR Hegnauer

This book is dedicated to those brave Cinderellas
who dared to step onto the stage with me and let me wave
my Modern Fairy Godmother wand over them.

Contents

Foreword

—∞—

I asked members of my community what they wanted at an upcoming weekend retreat, and one specific request surprised/ didn't surprise me: *Bring back Joanna Bloor.*

It was a surprise because Joanna worked magic at two previous live events my company hosted. We've also done several free Zoom workshops with her, and she and I even co-taught a course, "How to be self-promotional."

I thought my people had gotten their Joanna fix and were excited to meet new, amazing, life-changing people.

Nope.

And I was also not surprised because Joanna is like a glittery buzzsaw that cuts through all the unspoken, out-of-control BS in the workplace. She gets you out of the three career danger zones: You're bored, you're scared, or you're stuck.

How? She's honed in on one simple and universal problem and solution (and executives everywhere pay her an eye-popping hourly rate to get coached on this.)

Problem: Most decisions about your career are made in rooms you are not in.

Solution: Train people how to talk about your unique skills and genius and the things you *want* in the future so that you have an *advocate in that room.*

When you look at the problem from this point of view and go through all of Joanna's proven methodology, something that feels very outside your control suddenly becomes very inside your control.

Tell me, is that not just so f'ing refreshing to hear!?!?!?!?

It's like what people say about "luck." Yes, luck (and privilege) helped me raise venture capital, despite an astounding 98% gender funding bias against women.

But I also put myself in a position to benefit from that luck. I went to every awkward networking event and charged high-end conferences to my credit card.

Later, I hosted dinners in my house to help other female founders access desperately-needed networks.

Every single person who has ever funded me came out of one of those situations. They were someone I already had a long-standing relationship with.

So yes, I had luck. I met the amazing Joanna Bloor somewhere along the adventure I chose.

And I also practiced what she taught me: I got clear on my unique genius, found the people who could amplify it, and convinced them to invest (literally or figuratively) in future me.

And as they say, that has made all the difference.

Do you see why my audience can't get enough of Joanna? As it turns out, a Joanna fix is all about the excitement of meeting new amazing, life-changing people: because my people get to meet their future selves.

You are so lucky to have *Tales of Potential* in your sweet hands. You are holding life-changing magic.

Now go on, and learn how to wield it. My friend Joanna will teach you how.

Sarah Lacy
Author of *A Uterus Is a Feature, Not a Bug: The Working Woman's Guide to Overthrowing the Patriarchy*

Introductions

I'm Joanna, and I'm a speaker known for transforming the stories people tell about themselves.

Here's how the transformation goes: a person comes up on stage and tells me about what they do professionally. I listen. Then I reflect a new narrative back to them. And it blows their mind.

Story transformation isn't always what I was known for. So, how did I get here? What led to me doing something so extraordinary for a living?

Well, the first transformation I made to someone's story of their potential was a happy accident.

But as you'll soon see, it changed everything.

★ ★ ★

Before I continue, let's turn the tables for a minute and talk about you, the person I wrote this book for.

This book is for you if…

> …you know you're destined for more incredible things but feel unseen and have impostor syndrome, too.

> …you lead a team and want to lead meaningfully and not just manage.

> …you want to help someone who is brilliant but plagued with self-doubt.

> …you took a risk on a dream but ran into some harsh realities and need some inspiration to stay the course.

> …you have a friend who's said, "Don't sit next to Joanna at dinner if you don't want your dreams to come true." And you're terrified and curious about what that means. (Why? Because I've helped.)

Every one of you will find hope and strategies for turning your potential—and your team's potential—into your future.

Now, back to the story of my first story transformation.

It was 2015, and I was running a workshop for a team at Microsoft designed to help attendees understand how best to share their value with others.

The key lesson I was trying to teach was that manifesting ambition, individually and as a team, requires you to be clear about the value of the Future You.

That seems easy enough, right? Well, let me tell you, it wasn't.

I asked the participants, "Who do you think the 'Future You' is?" As our first step to unpacking that question, I had everyone write down three things that made them uniquely awesome.

Soon, I noticed a woman in the front row. Let's call her Jenny. Jenny's piece of paper was blank, and so was her face.

I quietly walked up to her and asked if I could help. She explained that she couldn't think of anything that made her uniquely awesome. She was stuck. There was defeat in her eyes.

I asked her about the accomplishments she was proudest of and where she hoped to have an impact in the future. As we chatted, a story about how brilliant, curious, customer-centric, and collaborative Jenny was started to take shape in my head.

It was a brief, compelling tale about her future potential that might be helpful to others. And as soon as the story formed, the words fell out of my mouth.

That's when Jenny started to cry.

She cried because this was the first time someone had told her, in a meaningful way, that she mattered. The entire room went silent as she spoke. We were stunned. Eventually, someone softly asked, "Can you do that again, but for me?"

This moment was tinged with magic, but what I had done was simple: I'd told a story. It wasn't about who Jenny had been but about who she could be in the future. It was a narrative of her potential.

Jenny will never forget it, and neither will I.

That day, I learned that even hardworking, ambitious, and conventionally successful people have a deep, unfulfilled need for transformational stories—and that this work was my future.

Since that fateful conversation, I've transformed thousands of stories.

Cristina, the entertainment executive at 21st Century Fox, dreamed out loud of shifting into the technology space—because "tech doesn't know how to tell stories." Cristina became the CMO at Salesforce.org, and that's just the beginning of her dreams coming true.

I once led a session with a roomful of US Army officers. They told me, with stern faces and arms crossed, how they were already experts in spotting and promoting potential.

But then I taught them about the "room you're not in" factor. And by the end of the day, the room's impact on military careers was all they could talk about. (You'll learn about this "room" later in the book.)

Steve Cakebread was the CFO of YEXT when he called me to ask, "Can you help me help them?" I giddily answered, "Yes!" and said, "Hold up, who am I helping and why?"

He had a male-dominated organization that needed more than just "women's programming." Our work together helped Steve turn empowering into an active word, something much more than a label.

I'll never forget sitting across the table from Leslie DeHoff, a Partner at Ernst & Young, and telling her to "stop being boring because you're not." I keep pushing her out of her comfort zone, and she keeps asking me back.

Hundreds of brave souls at conferences like TED, Women in Product, The TOIGO Foundation, the PGA Tour, and Content Asia chose to get up on stage, and they let me take their stories from boring to brilliant.

I've had eye-opening (and sometimes eye-watering) conversations about potential with individuals and teams from around the globe: Singapore, Australia, Germany, Holland, the UK, Israel, and Mexico. Their profiles range from a graduating high school senior to the COO of a major financial firm in Hong Kong.

I've learned from every one of them that they want to be seen and valued for their potential.

What Keeps us
Telling the Wrong Story?

Thousands of transformations later, I'm still amazed at how hard it is for people to tell anything but the most generic stories about themselves.

Like Jenny at Microsoft, most of us don't know how to talk about our potential. It's as though we're all stuck on the exact first step that she was at the workshop, unable to name three things that make us uniquely awesome.

As I see it, two main obstacles keep us stuck on what, in my mind, is the wrong story about ourselves. They are 1) our near-exclusive focus on the past and 2) our brain's tendency to make sh*t up.

1. We focus on the past.

We expect people to figure out our potential based on our stories from the past. It's not our fault that we do this; this is what we've been taught to do in the workplace.

Think about the times you offered yourself up to be chosen for a future role; by colleagues, hiring managers, or customers. Am I right that you tend only to tell the story of your past—your work history, challenges, and successes—and leave your audience guessing the rest?

We're similarly past-obsessed when we seek out people to join the team, lead a team, or collaborate on a project.

The tools and frameworks we use to guide our decisions focus only on past accomplishments. Look at resumes, performance reviews, titles, career paths, and job descriptions. Notice how they all look backward?

But data about the past, in and of itself, is insufficient to inform future potential.

Think about it. Isn't your value to a company, a team, based on who you'll be in the future? How you'll contribute tomorrow? What you'll perform next week, next quarter?

If our work is about influencing future outcomes, why are we only telling the past half of the story? And if you're in the selection seat, why are you making decisions based on such a limited dataset?

2. We make sh*t up.

Also, as humans, we tend to fill in the gaps when we're missing information, and aren't even conscious of how much we're doing this.

We habitually take keywords and data points and craft a story in our heads about who we believe the person is going to be.

Who was the last person you met that made you think, "Gosh, I'd sure like to hang out with them again"? You had, at most, partial input from this person before you drew that conclusion. How did you dream up a future with this person? By making up the missing pieces.

Now think about when you and the team you were on were doing your best work. I'll bet you had a clear and compelling story about why you needed each other and what you set out to accomplish (as did everyone else.)

But chances are, the understanding was implicit. Again, each team member had partial input, filled in the gaps, and made up a story about a future with each other.

Don't you want to make sure you've got a say in what others talk about when they're discussing the "future you"? Both as an individual and as a team?

Change is rapid, and we're saturated with options in the workplace. Do we have the luxury of trusting that someone's made-up story is close enough to ours?

We're overdue for a transformation of how we tell our stories about our future—and how we listen for stories about each other's futures.

We must say goodbye to the wrong stories and hello to our Potential Tales.

Cinderella: The Ultimate Wrong Story Transformation

To my utter delight, people perk up whenever I talk about my work. The subject of transformation resonates deeply—we want to tell stories based on the future, but we just don't know how to start.

That's why you, dear reader, are holding this book in your hands: so you can learn to tell Potential Tales, just like I do.

I wanted the teaching in this book to be fun. I also wanted it to make sense and be actionable. So, I thought long and hard about the people I've helped. I wondered aloud whose transformed story would offer the kind of gasp-worthy moments on the page that I create in person.

I'm pleased to bring you the oldest, the most misunderstood tale of potential I can think of. It's a fictional one from your childhood. Maybe someone read it to you at bedtime, or perhaps you watched one of several iconic movie versions, but either way, it's one you know well, or at least you think you do.

In case you hadn't already guessed, it's the story of Cinderella!

You probably think of her as a young woman who fell on hard times, got misused, but then caught a super lucky break. Fair enough.

Now, please imagine Cinderella as a modern-day, real-life person. And ask yourself these questions.

What would you hire her to do if she walked into your office today?

Would you hire her at all?

If her resume went through your applicant tracking system, would she even make it into the consideration set?

Most importantly, what's the story you're making up in your head—the room she's not in—about Cinderella?

The most common answer I get is this: "She's kind and pretty and has a great attitude, and I'd hire her for an entry-level position. Otherwise, she's not that impressive." Sometimes I hear something harsher. "She's pathetic and needed rescuing to create a better life; I wouldn't hire her at all."

Well, just wait until I work my transformation magic! You will not believe the brilliance you've missed in Cinderella all this time when I present my reframe, her Potential Tale.

This book has three parts: The Now You, The Near You, and The Future You. They correspond to the parts in the fairy tale before Cinderella meets the Fairy Godmother, the night of the royal ball, and the "happily ever after."

As the reframed story unfolds, I want you to see how Cinderella is—like you and like Jenny at Microsoft—full of unrecognized potential. And by seeing that you have the wrong story in your head about Cinderella, I hope you'll see how *your* story could be transformed, too.

The two things are closely intertwined. So closely, in fact, that I'm going to start each chapter with something I already know about you and connect it with a reframed scene or story element from the fairy tale.

And along the way, I'll present some real-world ideas that will inspire you to be more like Cinderella and put the learning into action. I want you to be empowered to get to whatever your equivalent of the "royal ball" is.

Your future is the story of potential, and that story needs to be correct to make your dreams come true.

Shall we get going?

The Cinderella You Know

I'm so excited to go on this story transformation journey with you. To be sure we're starting on the same page, I invite you to take a step back with me. Let's revisit the Cinderella story as we know it.

Once upon a time, there was a beautiful, sweet, orphaned maiden named Cinderella. She spent her days doing whatever chores her poor, twice-widowed stepmother Madame Tremeaine (or her two ugly stepsisters) gave her—with a bit of help from her friends, the mice and birds.

The prince of their kingdom was pressured to choose a bride and was determined to break from tradition. Hence, a royal ball was planned, and all the kingdom's young women were invited.

The stepmother excitedly readied gowns for the occasion—but only for her two daughters. To everyone's surprise, Cinderella appeared on the big night wearing a dress she and her friends had lovingly sewn from bits and bobs. She was ready to go.

The stepmother was enraged! And the stepsisters promptly tore Cinderella's dress to shreds.

Soon after, Cinderella fell to the ground, with her animal friends nearby, and wept beside squash vines. Then, she heard, "What's wrong, my dear?"

The voice belonged to none other than the Fairy Godmother! And with the wave of her wand, this Fairy Godmother turned a pumpkin into a coach, the animals into coachmen, and outfitted Cinderella with a shimmering gown and glass slippers.

Before the coach took off, the Fairy Godmother warned Cinderella of the one rule: leave the palace by midnight. That's when the magic would end.

Within minutes of her arrival, the prince spotted Cinderella and asked her to dance. The two proceeded to chat in private, and the prince was smitten. But then, ding dong ding dong, the clock struck midnight.

Cinderella took off running. When she got halfway down the staircase, one of her glass slippers fell off. She briefly paused but left it behind.

The prince was devastated. But the next day, he got an idea: he'd use the slipper to find the young lady! Soon, his attendants were traveling door-to-door, hosting try-ons and searching for the person whose small foot fit the shoe.

The stepmother heard the news and locked Cinderella up in the attic. But just as the attendants were leaving their house, Cinderella turned up; the mice and birds had helped free her. And she proved to everyone that she was "the one."

Cinderella and the prince married. And they lived happily ever.

The lesson you were taught from this tale is to be a good, cheerful girl who's always nice to everyone. Work hard. Really hard. If you do, there's a chance an influential person or two will see you, rescue you, and change your destiny. That's how success happens. Now go, dream on.

Well, excuse me. That is so NOT the point as I see it!

I have a completely different perspective, which we'll explore in the following chapters. In Cinderella, I see a character who is not "pathetic and kind" but is instead "proactive and strategic."

Here, let me give you a taste of what's to come. You're about to find out how Cinderella:

* Learned to move away from being a Get Sh*t Done girl

* Operated from a core value of generosity and kindness

* Cultivated the assistance of her squad

* Understood how to help people want her for what she wanted to be wanted for

* Played the long game and didn't shortcut the process

* Had a vision for who she wanted to be

* Knew how to be seen

* Had a knack for being her authentic self

Prepare to be amazed.

Tales of Potential
Discovery Experiments

Whenever a new idea inspires me, I ask, "So what's next? How do I implement this idea?"

It's very likely you'll get inspired to take action before you finish reading the last page. So I designed *Tales of Potential Discovery Experiments* to go with each chapter.

Each one includes four sections: Idea, Experiment, Amplify, and Invest. In short, they answer "What's next?" and "How?" for you, a modern leader (or would-be leader) learning from a fairy tale, and living and working in the real world.

If you'd like to get a sneak peek at the discovery experiments now, scan the QR code or go to talesofpotential.com/discover.

PART 1

The Now You + Cinderella

Time to jump in! As our first step, I want to introduce you to a framework I borrowed from a business strategy. I use it to help people figure out how to navigate their professional future.

The framework boils down to three simple questions. I want you to ask yourself:

★ How much of your resources are you applying to what needs to be done today to complete current commitments?

★ How much of your resources are you investing in projects looming on the six-to-twelve-month horizon?

★ And finally, how much of your resources are you investing in the future?

Your resource is your time.

And as the CEO and Founder of You, Inc., if you're only investing in what needs doing today, you'll find it hard to build a future.

When I work with clients, their time investment strategy is one of the first things I need to understand.

★ What's going on now? (This is The Now You).

★ What's happening soon, and how do we need to prepare for it? (This is The Near You).

★ What do you want to happen in the future? (This is The Future You).

As you'll see, the partnership between Cinderella and the Fairy Godmother was no different. If Cinderella had only focused on her "needs to be done today" list, we'd have a different story.

Actually, I'd argue we wouldn't have a story to reframe at all.

So jot down your answers and let your reframe begin.

Don't Be a
Get Sh*t Done Girl

———— ∞ ————

Maybe we've never met, but I know that you and Cinderella have one big thing in common: you get sh*t done. A lot of sh*t done.

You do this in all aspects of your life—school, home, family, parenting, community, volunteer gigs, and on and on—but most especially at work.

You do it to prove yourself. You do it for the reward—let's say, a raise to go along with a spot on the team with the juicy, strategic project—that's surely waiting on the other end.

And you do it to the point that getting sh*t done is what you're known for.

I call people like this Get Sh*t Done (GSD) girls, and I'm certain you are one of them. Yes, even if you don't consider yourself a girl.

No, you're not a slacker. Yes, your effort is entirely admirable. And yet I'm afraid that you, my dear, are courting disappointment.

Because when you're a GSD girl, you're not teaching people to value you. You're teaching people to give you more sh*t to do.

Let me illustrate my point using Cinderella as an example. She was all about getting sh*t done.

Clean the hearth!
Cook the food!
Fix my hair!

If someone asked her to do something, Cinderella always said yes.

The family expected Cinderella to complete each project with little to no complaint. Just make it happen, they would demand. They gave her fewer resources with every project and expected her to prove that she could handle it.

And handle it, she did, to the point that they trusted she could always figure it out. So why would the family ask for anything different?

Take a moment and imagine Cinderella was working for you.

Whatever task you give her she takes on with grace and delivers the project on time, under budget, and perfectly. You have someone on your team who can make the impossible happen and happen every single time like magic.

Wouldn't you keep giving her things to do? Wouldn't you start to trust that you could hand one project after another to this brilliant person?

Getting sh*t done is a critical part of a job. It's what builds trust and confidence in you. But at a certain point, if people only know you for getting it done, don't be surprised if they keep asking you to perform more GSD magic-making.

And if they only know you for your ability to *execute*, they're not going to know you for your ability to *think*. You won't get to be the person who decides strategy, aka the one who chooses what sh*t gets done.

I'm sure it stings to hear this. You probably had no idea your hard work was going against your desire to be valued. That's okay. We can solve this problem.

Acknowledgment is the first step. Know that your value is not only your ability to crank sh*t out. It's also your sense of how, when, and why you approach a task.

Your second step is to start telling others about your approach's how, when, and why. Teach people how you think as much as what you do, and then you'll be known for both.

And that's sharing your magic.

How to re-tell a tale of the GSD girl

If you're a leader, you might have recognized a Cinderella (or GSD girl) on your team. And yes, there is such a thing as a Get Sh*t Done Boy. They come in all shapes and sizes.

I presume you have a high level of trust in this person. Your GSD person might even love that you trust their ability to make things happen.

Next time you're looking at who's ready for promotion—or who might be the right person for a new role—I want you to consider your Cinderella team member. Are you only thinking about them as someone who can get sh*t done? If so, are you possibly keeping them by the hearth because your household won't run well without them?

I challenge you to think of their potential differently. Better yet, invite your GSD person to a conversation about their ambitions.

Trust + Potential = Awesome.

Ready to implement this idea? I'll guide you through it.
Go to talesofpotential.com/discover

Make the Best
Out of Bad Bosses

What's the number one reason people seek to change roles? Yup, you guessed it—it's the boss.

Kind as she was, we can assume that Cinderella did not love working for her stepmother. Then why didn't Cinderella just exclaim, "I QUIT!" and walk out the door? Sure, she'd be walking away from her family home, but couldn't she get room and board elsewhere?

She stayed because she was weak. That's what most of us assume.

Worse, she seemed to take the stepmother's verbal abuse and irrational behavior in stride. Didn't she break into song periodically?

No wonder Cinderella's tale of potential often starts with a shake of the head and sentences like, "She's a bit pathetic."

But look more closely, and you'll see she understood something that kept her from screaming inwardly every day. Take a pause and examine Cinderella's narrative about her future.

While her situation was terrible, Cinderella was brilliantly strategic about her work for the Family Tremaine. What we miss in the story is a playbook on how to take a terrible situation, a terrible boss, and turn it around.

I'm not joking when I say that I value this skill set so much that, given a choice, I've often sought out stepmother-type bosses.

Let me show you the opportunities I see in how Cinderella approached her work and even cherished working for her lousy boss.

1. **You have a boss who doesn't care how; they just want it done.**

   Instead of just meanness and a lack of investment or clarity, I see the upside in this boss of complete and utter autonomy. Seize this freedom, especially if you're looking for a role where you get to develop and implement a plan. No wonder Cinderella sang all the time. She took the demands of her family and created her own agenda.

2. **You have a boss who changes their mind a lot or lacks focus, makes irrational and inconsistent decisions, and is also a control freak.**

   I'm sorry; this one is a bummer. But think longer-term here. Use this chance to build your "top challenges I've navigated" portfolio, and become a pro at recognizing behavior patterns, redirecting difficult conversations, and making notes of the survival strategies you develop.

If you want to be in a leadership role, you'll one day be glad you got a crash course in doing hard things and having hard conversations.

We all know Cinderella ultimately wanted a different future for herself. But, instead of getting angry or breaking down in tears, it's clear Cinderella put all of her "how to deal with difficult situations" into a file for herself. So, when it mattered, she had something to reference and fuel the confidence to make the right decision.

3. **You have a boss who's somehow all those things and then some?**

Here's where Cinderella teaches you the ultimate lesson. This type of boss is a wealth of leadership anti-examples: call her the Tor-Mentor. Working for the stepmother helped Cinderella understand what makes her say "Hell no," and she let that inform what she wanted to say "Hell yes!" to.

Cinderella was far from stupid about the potential of her next opportunity AND the team she'd be working with. I'd add that seeing the "what not to do" playbook helped her create her "what to do" playbook.

As we know, Cinderella's next role moved her from individual contributor to leader almost overnight. She needed to fully form her authentic leadership style before moving from mopping floors into what was, for all intents and purposes, the kingdom's C-Suite.

Having a lousy boss often helps you craft your leadership style. You can create your unique and authentic playbook as you craft your path forward. The clearer you are about what kind of leader you are, the easier it'll be for others to opt in to working with you. And they will love it.

Working for a challenging boss is never easy. It wasn't for Cinderella, who dealt with relentless pressure to produce and incessant tongue-lashing. Of course, she didn't relish that part.

But she saw possibilities in her situation, not just blockages. That's why she worked with a smile.

Actively participating in learning, rather than sinking into muck and despair, laid the foundation for seizing a life-changing opportunity later.

So, think about it. That lousy boss you've got might also be the doorway to a bigger future for you.

How to re-tell a tale of leadership.

None of us thinks we're as bad a leader as the stepmother. And yet, every one of us has worked with someone who was that bad. The math doesn't quite work out. I'm sorry to tell you this, but someone somewhere has decided you're a terrible boss, just as someone somewhere thinks I was a lousy boss.

Your team chooses to work with you as much as you choose to work with them—but we forget this when we land leadership roles. Opting in to someone's potential is a bi-directional decision.

So how, as a leader, can you ensure the story of your potential is the best it can be?

1. Be like the Stepmother. Be consistent.

Cinderella knew who she was choosing; the stepmother was clear about where she stood. Now, does that permit you to be mean? Of course not. But when they don't know who will show up, the people working with you don't know how to react. So figure out what your leadership framework is, share it, and show up consistently.

2. While it's about you, it's also not about you.

I'm about to contradict the advice I just gave you, but stick with me; it'll all make sense.

Ask the individuals on your team what kind of leader they need you to be for them. Do they need:

* **A Coach Leader**—someone who can lock arms with them, give them lots of feedback and encouragement and show them how to create their future?

* **A Patron Leader**—someone who can riff on their ideas and help them see what possibility might look like?

* **Or an Investor Leader**—someone who treats them as the expert that they are, and only gets involved when there are obstacles they can't solve themselves?

Coach Leaders are great for someone who wants attention that's hands-on; for someone who doesn't, it might feel like micromanaging. Patron Leaders are great for someone who wants a partner to bounce ideas off; for someone who doesn't, it might kill their confidence as their ideas are never good enough. Investor Leaders are great for someone who has a vision and wants to be empowered to run with it; for someone who doesn't, it might feel lonely.

Figure out your framework, share it, show up consistently, AND leave space to co-create a leadership style that works for them.

3. **You don't have to be everything to everyone.**

When I say co-create, I'm not advocating that you be excellent at every style of leadership. That's such an unfair expectation! In fact, the best leaders I know are clear about where they're strong and where they're weak.

If your style tends toward an Investor Leader, find other people who can play different roles for your team. Just like your people can't be one-size-fits-all, neither can you. Diversity in thinking isn't limited to the builders and creators of the future; it's also essential for leadership styles.

Diversity of leadership thinking + potential = Awesome.

Bonus Questions

As you create your leadership playbook, I challenge you to make it consistent across all the groups of people opting into your potential.

- ★ How does your team perceive your potential?

- ★ How do your peers and colleagues perceive your potential?

- ★ How does your boss perceive your potential?

I know that's a lot to consider—leadership isn't for the faint of heart—but I guarantee your playbook will become the opposite of "How to Be a Lousy Boss." Your's will be a holistic blueprint for becoming a leader worth admiring.

And why, my ambitious friend, would you want to be any other kind of leader?

Ready to implement this idea? I'll guide you through it.
Go to talesofpotential.com/discover

Take a Walk in
Their Shoes Instead

Let's say you've learned some valuable life lessons from a toxic boss you loathe. You're even glad for the opportunity for self-discovery. (Congratulations. That's remarkable.)

But part of you is still screaming mad, and that's sucking the life out of you. Now what?

I know a surefire way to get on with it. It's simple. And while it's not easy, it worked well for Cinderella.

What you do is take a walk in your boss's shoes.

Skeptical? Fair enough. Want to see my theory in action before you jump on that advice? No problem. Because if there was ever a great example of a toxic boss, Cinderella's stepmother is it.

She's mean and petty; she backstabs and has no problem sending other people down the river for personal gain. She's jealous and not even ashamed to show it. It's easy for us to loathe her.

What had life taught this grand lady?

For context, she lived in those times when a woman's fate was determined mainly by her circumstances. As a young woman, she was titled and even rich—but just as soon as her husband died, she tumbled down the social ladder.

She had few opportunities and two young daughters to look after. So, what does she do but look for a new husband?

She succeeds at this. Yes, it meant remarrying a widower and caring for yet another daughter. But she got back the security she craved. At least for a minute, until Cinderella's papa died, and she became a widow once more. And this time, she's gone BROKE.

Let's take a moment and move this story into the real world.

What if one of your friends experienced this type of situation? She started with every luxury imaginable and had it torn away from her. She picked herself up (and the kids, too) and got back on her feet, only to be knocked down again.

Would you be lecturing her gently about being kinder, or would you be hugging her and handing her a frozen margarita? Would you point out how mean she was, or would you ensure the girls had other places to get help?

But alas, in this story, no squad shows up for Madame Tremaine. Alone, probably angry, and terrified of the unknown future, she does what every person does in that situation. She tries to control anything she can and protect everything important to her.

So, in the wake of everything, ensuring the prosperity of her two biological daughters becomes her mission. Cinderella, the stepchild, is a liability in her eyes. So she commits to squeezing as much work out of her as possible.

I'm not saying this is a forgivable approach. But it is understandable. Madame Tremaine was playing a short game driven by the need for power in a world full of ambiguity.

It's also no wonder the stepsisters, taking cues from their mother, hoard their resources and don't think twice about treating Cinderella poorly. For the three of them, it's all about the now—take what you can because you never know what tomorrow will bring, and in any case, there's not enough to go around.

Now it's confession time. I've not only worked for toxic bosses but I've also been the toxic boss.

In both cases, there was more to the story than people thought. My toxic behaviors were usually motivated by fear, just as Madame Tremaine's were. The same goes for the toxic bosses I worked for. They, too, were afraid.

Behind toxic behavior at work is a fear-filled story inside a person's head.

Cinderella seemed to get this dynamic without anyone explaining it. And she tried to understand where her stepmother was coming from rather than feeling righteous in her loathing.

Maybe you're thinking, "Good for her, but I'm not like that."

Oh really? But you can be. Just remember that when you are sick of silently screaming at your boss (not just the current one, but also that old boss who wronged you a few jobs ago), so tired that something must give, you have a choice.

You can take a deep breath, get curious about what you don't know about them, and be open to learning. You can practice walking in the other person's shoes, one step at a time.

Eventually, you'll find that you've opted out of silent screaming just as Cinderella did.

How do we know this? There are two versions of the end of Cinderella's story. One where she gets revenge and eyes get plucked out by vultures (ugh). The other is where Cinderella is full of compassion and kindness.

I don't know about you, but I know which ending I prefer. While revenge might feel great, we all know there's a price.

So take a beat, like Cinderella did. Ask yourself what backstory of fear and short-term thinking might be manifesting this madness.

Your freedom waits on the other side, and it is 100% worth it.

How to re-tell a tale of vulnerability.

Keep in mind that we all have bruises. Like Madame Tremaine, we've all had emotionally difficult experiences, and these experiences color how we lead others.

Madame Tremaine's past led her to choose a defensive and protectionist strategy toward her family's future, but imagine if she had taken a beat, sat down with the entire team, and said,

"Hey. This situation we're in, it's rough. We're going broke, and I'm worried about how you will all survive if anything happens to me. You know what, though? I have some ideas on how we can navigate the future and make our dreams come true even with the mess we're in. Can we talk?"

I can only imagine how different the story would have been for everyone involved. Madame Tremaine gets to be the mother-in-law of the future queen of fairy tale land, right?

You've heard the brilliant Brene Brown talk about vulnerability in her teaching. I'd suggest this is one of the perfect examples of how we, as leaders, can help our teams tell better stories of potential about us.

When people opt in to the potential Future You, everyone wins.

Vulnerability + Potential = Magic.

Ready to implement this idea? I'll guide you through it.
Go to talesofpotential.com/discover

More Paths = More Options

Sometimes you get a decent or even an outstanding boss. But unfortunately, the role you've got is some combination of soul-sucking, tedious, and demeaning.

You probably think that being in these jobs is a waste of your time. That's not entirely true, though. Just like bad bosses don't necessarily make you stuck, imperfect roles don't, either.

If you know how to work magic, then every role you're in (and have ever had) will contribute to building your dream. And the magic only requires two simple things, two things you've already got: a dash of courage and the willingness to take notes.

But before I give you the five-minute lesson, I want to share the back story of how I arrived at my dream job.

Once upon a time, I sold expensive swimsuits in a small boutique.

Once upon a time, I inflated 1,000 party balloons.

Once upon a time, I booked travel for corporations.

Once upon a time, I led a project to build software for a media company.

Once upon a time, I was part of the team that wrote the industry-standard terms and conditions for online advertising.

Once upon a time, I cut pounds and pounds of carrots.

There was something I hated doing and something I loved doing in every position I had. Part of every one of those roles shows up in the work I do today.

I learned the power of empathy at the swimsuit store. Even in the digital age, knowing every airport code in the United States has come in handy more times than I can count. You get blisters if you try to inflate 1,000 balloons, but inhaling helium is never not funny.

We see Cinderella's time as a seamstress, cook, cleaner, or whatever ridiculous thing the family needed as a terrible time in her life. Who would want to do all those jobs? How could they be helpful?

She eventually found herself in line to be the queen of fairy tale land. How much better of a queen will she be with the experience from her past?

We all know the answer.

Every role has a lesson embedded in it. The key to success is to tease it out, to add it to all the other skills you have at your fingertips.

When interviewing for a job, did I share how I learned to store cut carrots, so they keep fresh longer? Not often. But did I share about working in a swimsuit store—where I handled repeated objections while trying to help women of all sizes feel good in bikinis—when I interviewed for a job in media? Yes.

And my unique perspective, skills, and understanding of what my customer needed helped the hiring manager recognize my potential as a salesperson even though I didn't meet his explicit qualifications. Telling the potential story of HOW I learned that empathizing with my customer was the key to being a good salesperson and made me memorable. The combination of recognizable and memorable ultimately got me the job.

Once, I interviewed with a CEO for a critical VP role. I needed to help this person see how I saw supply chain efficiencies in a digital world. So I referenced a book I'd read at age thirteen. (It was *Clever-Lazy: The Girl Who Invented Herself* by Joan Bodger.)

I shared with my potential boss how the story of invention resonated with me early and how it empowered me to look at every problem from many angles. For it's in finding the unexpected angle that breakthroughs manifest. I told him I thought his company needed a similar breakthrough.

Did he mock me for bringing up such an odd framework? Not at all. The CEO understood far more than just my past accomplishments—he understood my potential impact on the organization's future. All because, by using the tween book's framework, I was able to share how, why and what I thought about the problems they needed to solve.

I want you to revisit the roles you've had in the past—even the roles you've hated. Take inventory of the lessons and unique skills you've picked up.

Knowing what's on that list is bound to make you a better leader, team member, all-around better human, and in the long run, a better queen.

How to re-tell a tale of talent.

I get very excited when I speak to leadership about this particular idea. Why? Because if you get this right, you get to be a Modern Fairy Godmother (person/father) like me.

When hiring, how many of you are uninspired by the rote answers you get from, "So tell me about yourself?" Maybe that's the wrong question.

Imagine you prepped your candidates and shared with them how you want to explore lessons-learned from their various roles, and you're looking for stories and examples of skills they've developed that aren't in the job description.

Why is this important? Remember, candidates are already qualified if they have made it to the interview stage. Your job is not to validate their qualifications but to learn how they think.

I can't imagine you want a candidate to simply recite every step of what they did in the past. Rather, you want a candidate who'll take what they've learned in the past and apply it to YOUR organization's future.

Here's another idea. When someone completes a challenging task or navigates a complicated situation, don't just say, "Great job." Take a moment and give them the language they can use to describe the value of their contribution. Explain how brilliant they are to others (team members, future bosses, YOUR boss), so they can opt in to this person's potential.

Think about it. If someone works for you, you have a unique perspective on this person's future value. WHAT they've done and HOW they've done it is crystal clear to you. But it's often invisible to them.

So make a point of having these conversations. I promise they'll turn into some of the most delightful ones of your career.

Recognizable and memorable stories = Easier to see someone's future = Magic.

Ready to implement this idea? I'll guide you through it.
Go to talesofpotential.com/discover

Make it Easy to Opt In
to a Future With You

Your present: who and what you said yes to yesterday.

Your future: who and what you say yes to today.

And to make your dreams come true—to manifest your ambitions—you'll need people who buy into those dreams and create this future with you.

Here's an example. Remember how Cinderella injected song, light, and relentless optimism into whatever doldrum she faced?

I'm sure taking that approach made the minutes pass more quickly. But even more importantly, Cinderella made it easy for others to see what kind of day—and what kind of future—she wanted to create: one overflowing with kindness and generosity.

And how did the mice and birds respond? By wholeheartedly opting in to creating this reality with her. They sang with her and did chores with her, all without pay.

Not only did this teamwork move the needle on bringing Cinderella's future vision into reality pronto, but it also provided the foundation for future magic. No friends = no one to become coachmen!

At their best, ambitions are goals that create current and future opportunities for you, bring others on and produce results that delight everyone.

This definition shifts the narrative from an exclusively "me" focus ("What do I need to do for ME to succeed?") to an "us" focus ("What can I do for everyone to end up in a better place?") Generosity is embedded into this version of ambition like they were always supposed to be together.

Are you making it easy for people to opt in to a future with you—as Cinderella did for her critter friends?

Remember: there's no such thing as a dream coming true without others saying yes. So, the sooner you take that step, the sooner your beautiful future can arrive.

How to re-tell a tale of success.

As a leader, I've sometimes misinterpreted generosity as a lack of ambition. It took exploring the Cinderella story to realize I was wrong, especially in the context of teamwork.

Here's the thing about getting people to work well together: they only do it when they're opting in to each other's future ambitions.

Think about the time you've been on a team and thought, "Yes, I'd work with this group of people over and over again." What was the magic ingredient? You opted in to a future with them, and they chose a future with you.

Create a team that's all ambition-focused, and they'll have a selfish mindset.

Create a team that's all generosity-focused, and they'll have the Get Sh*t Done mindset we spoke of earlier.

Create a team that's both. That's when the magic happens now *and* in the future. And isn't your job as a leader to help your team make magic happen?

Generosity + Ambition = Magic.

Ready to implement this idea? I'll guide you through it.
Go to talesofpotential.com/discover

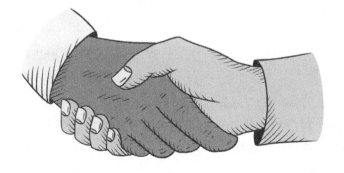

Ambition is What You
Want for YOUR Future

I have more to say about ambition.

The point of it isn't to elevate your standing among peers, gain status, and collect the accouterments (titles, awards, estates, investment portfolios, red carpet pictures with celebrities, charities named after you, etc.) to prove that you've "made it."

It isn't even to win the next promotion.

The point of ambition is to guide your choices—so you play a long game centered on what you most value. And ensure your actions have an impact.

Look closely at Cinderella's miserable days with her family. Was her ambition really to get a better life by using the only lever she had, aka the prince, as most people assume?

I don't think so.

For starters, Cinderella could have run away to get a better life. Or she could have dug for dirt, blackmailed her stepmother, and negotiated her release. Neither option is far-fetched; either one could have been quickly executed, and none involve the prince.

And yet, she stayed. She chose graciousness. She chose kind words even when talking to difficult people. All of this, long before a royal ball or the possibility of marrying the prince was on the horizon. And without another human to validate or reward her choices.

So, it's reasonable to conclude that Cinderella had priorities we hadn't recognized before. She must have taken her terrible job and made it meaningful for a reason, right?

Wonder what that reason could be? I have a hunch.

Take a moment to think about the leaders we admire most—those who work from their core values.

These leaders may have big-time job titles or influential status now. But did they wait for someone else to give them a title, status, or permission before they stood for something? I think not. To them, ambition is about acting on your beliefs and making a meaningful impact—whoever you are, whatever your title—even when the people around you make it super hard to do that.

Cinderella was ambitious in that same way. And my goodness, Cinderella was committed to playing the long game!

I'd argue that her ambition was to take this core concept of how to be—generous and kind—and spread it as far and as wide as she could.

Go back to who she is at her core. Cinderella was manifesting her ambitions even while her family treated her like a servant. Was her entire audience appreciative? No. But she found those who were and kept up her efforts.

Let's stretch our imaginations even more. Imagine Cinderella met someone other than the prince. Would she still get to manifest her ambitions in that scenario? Yes, absolutely.

Becoming the queen-in-waiting meant she had a platform and a whole kingdom to which she could teach her values. Her elevated status, I'd say, was a happy bonus, as much a benefit for the royal family and the kingdom as it was for her.

(That said, I'd like to think she delighted in donning a tiara every time she spoke to an audience! I know I would have.)

So now that I've shown you how ambition works—as a guide and a core-values compass—I want you to try filling in the blank below.

My ambition is to _____.

How to re-tell a tale of ambition.

Ambition is *the* potential tale I see heading in the wrong direction all the time.

Why? Because as leaders, we assume we know what someone's ambitions are. We get so excited about who this person could be that we forget to stop and ask the person what *their* aspirations are.

Ambition is as unique as someone's fingerprint.

Get it right, and you can make magic happen. Get it wrong, and it's akin to handing a team member a poisoned apple. Think about it, hasn't this happened to you? I know it has for me.

If I've got you thinking, "Oh! I should ask my team what their ambitions are," then you are on the right track. But a word of caution—you'll likely hear the following:

1. I want a promotion
2. I want a raise.
3. I want to learn and grow in my role.
4. I want to have an impact in my role.

In a world where we teach people that success is winning at the video game of life—level up and cheat code your way to the top—these answers shouldn't be a surprise. These ambitions aren't bespoke; they're what we've taught people to say.

So, take the time to ask them WHY they want this future. You'll be surprised by what you find out.

I've run into all sorts of situations where the expected and actual ambitions were out of sync.

Once, a newly minted executive asked me how to still be seen as ambitious by their leadership team without getting promoted.

"At this company, if you fly too close to the sun, you get burned and fall. I'm close enough to fulfill my ambitions and want to stay here," they said.

They worried that putting on the brakes would make people think less of them. And yes, the "sun" in this example was the founder. So we put together a plan that allowed them to have this tricky conversation with their manager.

In another scenario, I helped a leader who wanted to get promoted. He believed that without constant learning opportunities, he wouldn't succeed. So his manager struggled to find projects for him that looked like learning opportunities. This dynamic exhausted both of them.

Eventually, this leader realized that finding the learning opportunities he craved was his job, not his manager's. He also recognized that he was over-optimizing for potential and not the present, and as an executive, he needed to do both.

The promotion eventually happened, and he and his manager are now much more chill.

So remember: you and your team must uncover the truth of your ambitions to have a remote chance of making them true.

The clarity in Ambition = Possibility to make magic happen.

Ready to implement this idea? I'll guide you through it.
Go to talesofpotential.com/discover

Crush Corporate
Professional Loneliness

Now that I've had you reflect on your most authentic, profound ambition, I'm wondering: do you ever feel like you get in your own way?

If your answer is yes, you're certainly not alone. Many accomplished people have confided that the bigger the ambitions and wilder their dreams, the more they interfere with them.

Fortunately for you, Cinderella can teach you a brilliant workaround. She was quite skilled at solving this problem.

Eager to learn? Fantastic. But first, let's dig deeper into how this business of getting in your own way works. I'll use the stepmother as an example.

As you've already heard, Madame Tremaine had little support. And she saw the world, very understandably, through the lens of scarcity.

When her daughters got invited to the royal ball—a fantastic opportunity to manifest her ambition of setting them up for a good life—it didn't make her feel more fortunate. Instead, she felt agitated. She doubled down on controlling her resources and outcomes.

You can see how minimal support from others and a scarcity mindset create a vicious cycle.

Most of us fall prey to fixating on lack and scarcity. It's not a character flaw; human brains are wired to notice and hold onto data about potential danger (you may have heard the term "negativity bias" before).

This wiring keeps us safe from encroaching famine and tiger attacks. But the wiring won't keep us from getting in the way of our ambitions.

So, if you want better outcomes for yourself than Madame Tremaine's and you want to protect your ambition from sabotage, you must do as Cinderella did. You need to get yourself a squad.

Here are six key benefits Cinderella reaped from investing in a squad.

1. Squads pick you up when you're down.

The birds and the mice Cinderella befriended filled her days with song, dance, and laughter as she tackled one demeaning chore after another. And if she got a nasty tongue leashing by her stepmother, the squad stayed by her side for comfort.

2. **Squads rally around you to help.**

They were there before the royal ball when the dress was torn. They showed up when the stepmother locked Cinderella away to keep her from trying on the glass slipper. Cinderella never faced a crisis alone.

3. **You can show your squad all your flaws, and they'll still support you.**

Cinderella must have been melodramatic, crabby, or even a tad harsh sometimes. By sticking around, her squad taught Cinderella that her flaws don't define her.

4. **It's OK to cry in front of your squad.**

The fastest way to move on from a setback is often to surrender to our struggle and (momentary) despair. In the presence of her friends, Cinderella was able to go there.

5. **Squads never tell you what to do; they support you and are ambitious for your future.**

The birds and mice had a vision for Cinderella sharing her gifts of kindness, resourcefulness, and more. Not just with them, but on a much, much bigger scale.

6. **Squads invite authenticity.**

Cinderella cultivated a friendship with the birds and mice and got to lead her life with generosity—her core value. She got to be herself every day and be valued for it long before the ball, the prince, and happily ever after materialized.

Can you see, dear reader, how the squad had everything to do with Cinderella having a dream and pursuing it? Despite the overwhelming lack in her everyday life?

If it weren't for the squad, Cinderella may not have dared to get herself to the ball, leaned into the Fairy Godmother's magic, or dazzled the prince with her grace and inner strength.

Cinderella avoided the trap of proving her negativity bias right. She saw possibilities where others saw threats, thanks to her squad.

Imagining and leaning into a brighter future, the actual Future You, can be a lonely adventure. Especially if you're new to this way of thinking or new to exploring what your dreams even are.

When you have someone on your squad who believes in the Future You, manifesting that person becomes significantly easier.

I'm not saying your adventure is going to be easy. But with a squad, you've got people reminding you, "I've got you. And I know you can do this. Just move forward."

How to re-tell a tale of teamwork.

In one of my former leadership positions, I needed to budget for replacing every person on my team every 12-18 months per industry standards.

This company also had massive growth plans, which meant we'd need to constantly add more excellent people to the team. The team in question went from thirty to 300 people in three years.

Between the replacement and growth factors, I had a pretty sizable recruiting and retention math problem. I knew we'd need to create growth and development opportunities at an epic rate to keep up.

Our solution? We became the "farm team" for the company. I went to ALL the leaders in the organization and told them they could recruit from my team all day, every day, with our blessing and our assistance.

We also committed to vigorously identifying potential across our ranks. We brought people to the attention of other team leaders, people who, while their resumes might not show it, would be a good fit for the challenges they had in the future.

This recruitment strategy was a spectacular success. Many team members of mine found themselves on career adventures they couldn't have imagined and stayed at the company.

Other departments found talent that was curious and excited to work with them and came to the role with a unique knowledge set, making them valuable additions to the team.

Moreover, we found this tactic contributed to a dramatic increase in organizational empathy. We had former teammates throughout the organization who had real-world experience with our department's challenges. It meant that when we needed to collaborate cross-functionally, the experience was so much simpler.

Some seven years later, I understood that this approach created squads of cross-department teams—groups of people with a common thread and a common ambition. What's lovely to watch is that, even though some of them have moved on to different companies, the squads are still thriving. They're still cheering each other on, picking each other up, and frequently coming back together to create new futures.

As a leader, I challenge you to develop a better ambition to manifest.

Squads + Potential = Magic.

Ready to implement this idea? I'll guide you through it.
Go to talesofpotential.com/discover

You're Renting a Subscription to Their Future Time

At the beginning of this book, I asked, "If you met Cinderella in the real world and had a chance to hire her on your team, would you, and in what role?"

I imagined you agreed with the consensus that she'd be fit for an entry-level position at best. By now, you may be reconsidering your answer, if just a little.

Is it possible that the thinking that led to you getting Cinderella's story wrong intertwines with how you see limitations in your own potential and the possibilities for your future?

Unfair as it is, some humans have perception barriers to work through for their transformational capacity to be seen, even by themselves.

These perceptions are super challenging to change in the present tense.

That's why I want to teach you about "subscribing to each other's future time." It's a concept that will shift the way you see how collaborations form and the value you bring to them.

As someone in the modern working world, you have customers—your friends, co-workers, manager, and even your actual customers.

Horrible as they were, Cinderella's stepsisters were devoted customers who kept opting in to Cinderella (I mean, who wouldn't.) The stepsisters could easily picture how "renting Cinderella's future time" would result in great things.

Let's say that Cinderella grasped this concept and she mapped her existing skills in customer service to the job she dreamed of: queen.

She'd see that being the queen has everything to do with customer service.

While marrying the prince might sound like parties and diamonds, the reality of the queen's job is to be a servant of the people. In that role, your subjects are, in fact, your *customers*, and you need them to keep opting in.

(Take a spin through history, and you'll see that every revolution started with the people saying, "Yeah. No thanks. This isn't working. We don't choose you anymore.")

So back at home, the stepsisters' lost things were always found, their broken things were fixed, and dirty dishes became clean dishes. Cinderella didn't just complete tasks for her customers;

she also understood what made them happy and included small touches.

What's more, she increased her capacity to serve by bringing on a highly motivated team (yeah, the mice and birds.) And Cinderella delivered all this transformational work with a great attitude 99.9% of the time.

That's how Cinderella kept the stepsisters subscribing to her future time and opting in to who she was, unlike many real-life queens.

Are you starting to see what I see? With all that organization and thoughtfulness, Cinderella could absolutely scale her operation to the level of Chief Customer Experience Officer, aka queen of her kingdom!

When we look at matching roles to people through the lens of subscribing to each other's future time, we can bypass limited perceptions. And consider Cinderella for bigger and better collaborations.

Now back to you. Let's apply the same imagination exercise to your situation. What if *you* grasped the potential in the "future time subscription" you're selling right now? What could change if you chose to have a say in it?

To enter those dream collaborations, you'll still have to help others see what renting your future time could do for them. Your customers must opt in to you and what you have on offer.

But the first crucial step lies with you: to see the value of your future time inside who you are right now.

How to re-tell a tale of hiring.

The concept that "you are renting a subscription to your future time" is bi-directional.

YOU are renting a subscription to their future time.

THEY are renting a subscription for their future time TO you.

YOU are offering compensation and opportunity as payment for that subscription. You are offering a subscription to a future opportunity.

THEY are offering their time and brilliant mind as payment to you for compensation and the promise and potential of the opportunity.

YOU opt in to a future with them as much as they're Opting in to a future with YOU.

When you don't both want the same future, at least one person is bored, stuck, scared, or opting out.

That's why Cinderella ultimately opted out. Even though I'm sure the Family Tremaine didn't want her to.

But when what you opt in to is balanced on either side, all kinds of good things happen and become a happy dance.

Opting In = Magic.

Ready to implement this idea? I'll guide you through it.
Go to talesofpotential.com/discover

The Magic is Already In You

As we close Part 1 of this book, I want to shine a light on this simple but powerful idea—

You can do magic.

Magic isn't about skills and experience. Those are your tools.

Your magic is inside your brilliant imagination, which allows you to think of things that aren't yet here or events that haven't yet happened.

Your magic is also inside your capacity to collaborate with other humans and solve problems for each other.

Your magic is that unique intersection of what you've learned in the past, who you are today, and what you can do in the future.

By nature of being human, magic has been bestowed on you.

Now, for the magic to work, you need to:

1. Know what your magic can do.

2. Understand why other people might need your magic.

3. Make it possible for other people to tell you, "Yes, please. I want some of your magic."

Your answers will feed into what I call the Opt In Equation: what you want to be wanted for = what others want you for. When the equation works out, everything is awesome.

This awesome is possible for you and your team. When you learn to tell Potential Tales, the Opt In Equation becomes your way of life.

So, before you move on to Part 2, I encourage you to go back and review the Potential Tales. Take notes about the reframed Cinderella story that struck you the most. See if there's room to apply that awareness to your story and make amendments.

Because we're about to meet the Fairy Godmother, and you want to be ready for an even wilder tale of transformation than the one you've just heard.

PART 2

The Near You
+ Cinderella

So far, we've taken the "a bit pathetic and in need of rescuing" narrative of Cinderella and reframed it into "she had the potential to be something more, but she was stuck."

You've seen how she led an ambitious life from the start, applied the lessons she learned to a budding career in customer experience, and kept self-sabotage at bay by investing in a squad.

And I've shown you how to apply these ideas to get more from your role. Now.

Welcome to Part 2, The Near You. We've come to the magic-packed part of the fairy tale. It centers on the Fairy Godmother's appearance on the night of the royal ball.

All kinds of amazing things happen. And as the story goes, the Fairy Godmother gets all the credit, not our brilliant, curious ingenue.

One key idea I want you to take away from Part 2 is this: *magic requires participation.*

A Fairy Godmother can create all the opportunities in the world, but if the person she's transforming doesn't participate in the process, all you have is someone in a lovely frock sitting on their front lawn.

And you already know the story didn't stop there.

You're about to see how Cinderella opened doors of opportunity for herself with risk-taking, confidence, and being strategic in the face of uncertainty—and how you can do the same in the real world.

I'll say it again: magic requires participation. Anything can happen when you know how to participate (Opt In).

So, come along now. The Fairy Godmother magic is about to begin.

Determination
Needs a Focus Point

She's got her face in her hands. Tears are falling in big droplets from the cracks between her fingers, hitting the dark, damp ground. Cinderella has just broken down at the sight of her homemade ball gown, ripped to shreds at the hands of her stepsisters.

Then a little old lady pops out of the bushes and asks, "What's wrong, my dear?"

I have a question for you. If some crazy-looking lady popped out of the bushes while you were out for a walk, would you give her the time of day?

I'm not sure I would have stopped to chat, but Cinderella did.

Let's recall how Cinderella answers the Fairy Godmother's question.

Does she tell a rambling story of what a nasty and mean thing her sisters did, how ugly and jealous and entitled they are, how her stepmother gives them so much while treating her like a servant and giving her an impossible number of chores to complete every single day?

Not quite.

Did she mention how this is all so unfair, how nothing has been the same since Papa died, that there are no signs this misery will let up? And how she's missed this once-in-a-lifetime opportunity to reverse her misfortune, so now, she might be doomed forever?

No.

No, even though the Fairy Godmother asked her what was wrong. And a response like that would've been appropriate.

What did Cinderella say?

"I planned to go to the royal ball. I still want a chance to dance with the prince. But now, I have no dress to wear and no ride to the palace."

In the introduction to Part 2, I said that magic requires participation. Notice how Cinderella participates in it from her first conversation with the Fairy Godmother:

★ She leaves out any reference to how she got into this pickle. She blames no one, not even herself.

★ She never loses sight of where she was headed. She states what she wants and what just got in the way of making things happen.

Dear reader, this is why the Fairy Godmother could go straight into magic mode.

The clock was ticking, so neither of them wasted time looking backward; they'd sort things out and move forward instead. Right this instant.

The point is that if you have a goal, it helps to keep it firmly in sight. It also helps to articulate your goal—clearly!—to anyone who asks.

If you want a better future, figure out what it is and focus on it, even when it's tempting to dwell on the past. You'll be helping yourself *and* the people who can and want to help get you where you're trying to go.

(Otherwise, you might find yourself "magic-ed" to places you didn't intend to be.)

How to re-tell a tale of confidence.

When I'm interviewing executives about what they need to successfully add other executives to their team, it often boils down to what I call the Executive Intersection.

Does the individual have the experience we need to predict your future confidently, and does the individual have the ability to recognize and act on the right opportunities that manifest from that future?

Today's executive needs to be able to do both.

Cinderella, we've already established, is brilliant at both. Long game thinking, along with the courage to act in the moment. Fantastic. Hired!

Here's where I want to challenge your thinking.

What kind of actions are you rewarding?

What kind of actions are you penalizing?

If you're only rewarding success and penalizing failure, your team's potential future paths will become less innovative, safer, and predictable.

What you want on your team are people who think like Cinderella. People who think about the long-term impact of a project and act fearlessly in the moment when they must.

And to act fearlessly, they need to be confident in the future.

Ready to implement this idea? I'll guide you through it.
Go to talesofpotential.com/discover

You Should Break the Rules (When it's Called For)

—— ∞ ——

Contrary to popular belief, how we respond to rules isn't about personality. It's about agency, taking responsibility for our direction, and exercising discernment in any situation.

Don't believe me? Take a look at Cinderella.

She's generally considered a rule-following type; obedient, even.

She got an enormous amount of housework done with no complaints. But do you know what else is true? She recruited the critters. Cinderella did the work as told, but she subverted her stepmother's expectations that she'd suffer through the chores alone.

Cinderella minded and defied her stepmother all at once.

This discerning mindset toward rules had everything to do with participating in the magic that led her to meet the prince.

Think back to when the invitation to the royal ball arrived at the house. Cinderella asks her stepmother, quite explicitly, if she, too, was invited to this monumental event. Rather than give a direct answer, the stepmother just says, "Don't expect a new dress."

What did Cinderella conclude from this conversation? That if she supplied her own dress, she could go. So she got the job done. Not just once, but twice (if we give her credit for co-creating the magical outfit with the Fairy Godmother. And we should.)

As you can see, Cinderella is quite a bit more than meets the eye.

Now, I can hear you thinking, "I get that showing agency is a good thing, but in the real world, we have rules for a reason! I don't think my boss wants someone who's strategically naughty on our team." So let me talk about how rule-breaking and potential go together.

Situation 1:
Getting help when it wasn't allowed.

The last time I checked, teamwork and collaboration were pretty high on the list of attributes in a great teammate and leader. What does the success of a near-future project require? A person with the skills and ability to recruit others to help them! And in Cinderella's case, she accomplished this mission without even offering compensation. Impressive, no?

Situation 2:
Not taking no for an answer.

Granted, this one can be tricky. Leaders want someone who won't habitually push back or work around your nos. But if they're honest with themselves, they'll admit to wanting someone who'll question and work around *someone else's no* as needed. It's a bit of a double standard.

If you're a leader, I encourage you to celebrate when someone has figured out how to work around your no. Resist the temptation to punish them for it. Before you know it, you will need that same person to turn another person's no into a yes. So why not let them practice on you?

To manifest a new future, you must shift your thinking from "what should" to "what if"—and when the occasion calls for it, answer the "what if."

Even if it means breaking (some of the) rules, just as Cinderella did.

Re-tell the tale of rules.

Just because someone's more senior than you doesn't mean they know the right way of doing things.

We learn this as children when we realize our parents are just trying to figure things out. We understand this again as adults when we recognize that while our boss might have more context and experience in a situation, they, too, are just trying to figure out how to move forward.

You might be surprised to learn that my advice here for the real world is not to take Cinderella's path and always work around the rules. She shifted from the "what should" to "what if" thinking because she had no choice but to work around her boss.

I want you to START on Cinderella's path of coming up with creative solutions to obstacles. But unless you're planning on being fired (well, Cinderella quits, but you get the point), staying on that path without everyone on board with your new idea is terrible news.

Your ideas for the future are part of what makes you extraordinary. Just remember ideas need adoption as much as execution to succeed.

Ready to implement this idea? I'll guide you through it.
Go to talesofpotential.com/discover

Don't Just Transform—Inform

There are so many situations where the path forward is unclear. Situations like this can seem threatening, and many of us try in vain to keep them at bay.

Let me introduce you to a different way of thinking about ambiguity. One that, frankly, I find so much more fun, more enchanting, and more magical.

If you can't see a clear path forward, you find ways to use what you have in a way it wasn't intended.

Here's an example. In the brief moment Cinderella had with the Fairy Godmother, she saw this idea in action.

Pumpkin to coach.
Mouse to a horse.
Goose to the coachman.

The list goes on. I applaud the Fairy Godmother for creating a wonderful future Cinderella could never have anticipated from elements already in Cinderella's environment.

If you're working in an ambiguous world, this type of transformation is the way forward.

Every breakout innovation started as one thing but became another through a series of adjustments. Ask anyone who's had an impactful career, and they'll tell you, "I was this, and then something happened, so I adjusted."

I want you to notice how there's an idea and a *reaction to* the idea at play here. Just having the idea isn't enough for transformation. You have to get other people to say, "Yes! I see it too!"

In the Fairy Godmother's case, she transformed the pumpkin into a coach. Cinderella could see the before and after. Until that moment, Cinderella probably thought pumpkin = potential for a tasty pie. My guess is, from that magic moment onward, Cinderella looked at all squashes with an eye to potential transportation solutions.

Before the Fairy Godmother started her magic making, Cinderella couldn't "see" such a potential future. But it only took that first transformation for her to see this potential everywhere.

Instead of just sorting Cinderella out with a giant BLAMO and magic-ing everything from one state to another, she took Cinderella along on the transformative journey.

In doing so, she showed Cinderella how she created possibilities out of raw ingredients and an uncertain situation.

Re-tell the tale of transformation.

To see the capacity for one thing to transform means we see potential. That ability is worth a lot when the path forward is ambiguous and few in the room know what to do.

If you lead, one of the most powerful things you can share with your team is HOW and WHY you're thinking about change. When we're focused on the end state and not the process, our teams can't learn how to get there next time. You always want to empower them for next time.

This idea also applies to an individual. The magic of potential is in helping others to see what you do.

You might see your "pumpkin" self full of potential and the "coach" in all its sparkling glory. But if the other person has never seen your pumpkin become a coach, it will be impossible for them to imagine.

Remember, it's not your experiences, but THEIR experiences of what THEY see that create their transformation story.

Ready to implement this idea? I'll guide you through it.
Go to talesofpotential.com/discover

You Have to Have Courage to Get to The Next Level

─────────── ∞ ───────────

There are two ways to manage risk as you enter unfamiliar settings to uplevel your game.

1. Ensure you ask all the right questions and get all the correct answers in advance.

2. Show up, pay attention to what's working, and lean into action. Unknowns are par for the course.

Which way did Cinderella go on the night of the royal ball? Let's find out.

Seconds after producing a pumpkin-turned-carriage, the Fairy Godmother tells Cinderella to get in. And by golly, she does!

Now I don't know about you, but most people would be hard-pressed to trust a ride that, until two minutes ago, was a squash vine lying on the ground.

I mean, what if it magicked back while you were still inside? One's imagination could go off the deep end here. Everything from finding yourself on the side of the road covered head-to-toe in pumpkin goop to the potential of death by pumpkin squashing.

If I were in Cinderella's shoes, I would have looked at my Fairy Godmother and said, "Um. Very cool. But can you do that a couple more times? Also, how did you do that? Oh, and how long does the pumpkin stay that way? All night? 30 minutes?"

And besides the pumpkin-coach situation, a million things could have gone wrong with the whole getting-to-the-ball plan. If I were Cinderella, I'd have peppered the Fairy Godmother with a million more questions before agreeing to proceed.

But Cinderella chose to trust and bet on herself. She willingly leans into this dicey situation with a "launch first and problem-solve as we go" attitude.

With that, she makes her way to the ball! And, as you'll soon see, her brave adventure is only getting started.

Okay, so now, our heroine is inside the palace. And it's time to enter the ballroom and be "chosen" by the prince. Another key moment in Cinderella's story.

You might think the path to success was inevitable; once she walked into the ballroom, everything would be fabulous.

But walking through the doors into the ballroom was another act of bravery. Another moment of thinking on her feet and moving forward when the future was murky.

Let's assess the situation together.

First, Cinderella realizes she's got zero royal ball experience to draw on. She had no peers or mentors to quietly pull aside and ask, "Hey, what's the protocol here?"

And it's not like Cinderella has the option to whip out her phone and Google "royal ball best practices." Also, Cinderella has spent most of her life cleaning, cooking, and sorting out other people. She has not done deportment classes like many of the other attendees had. If you think about it, she must've had imposter syndrome raging in her head.

Have you had to walk into a room like that? What would you have done if you were in her fancy glass slippers?

Well, we know that Cinderella, badass that she is, sees that this occasion calls for theatrics. She ups the drama ante and makes herself 10x more visible than before. Why?

Because Cinderella quickly gathered real-time data and figured that, to be chosen, she needed to be seen. Instead of hiding and hoping, she made a grand entrance down the staircase.

So now you know. Without a doubt, Cinderella chose option two: pay attention to what's working and then go!

I know that being brave like her isn't easy. But here's the thing; you can't get all the answers in advance when the situation is dynamic and complex. And every single up-leveling opportunity is dynamic and complex like that, my dear reader.

So, option one was never available to Cinderella. It isn't an option for you, either.

Cinderella's attention could've been on what might go wrong (which was a lot). But she zeroed in on what can go right, which made the magic happen.

On your way to dancing with the prince, whatever that means for you, you'll be navigating a ton of unknowns. Sometimes the stakes will be high, yet you'll have little instruction or experience to draw on. So cultivate courage; it's an essential ingredient in leveling up.

To get to the next level, you must know what intelligence and courageous risk-taking look like in action. And lucky for you, Cinderella has just shown you how it's done.

Re-telling the tale of courage and potential.

Protocols and "how things should be done" are social constructs designed by the people in power.

I learned this lesson when I moved from England to America at age fifteen. My Cinderella moment was walking into a Texas high school.

I had been attending a "Hogwarts without boys or magic" in England but suddenly found myself in a version of "Friday Night Lights." I went from uniforms and hockey sticks to jeans and cheerleaders. Yes, it was a shock.

Fortunately, I showed up in Texas in the equivalent of a ball-gown: a very clipped British accent. People kept saying, "I just love the way you talk." And the reaction to how I spoke gave me almost instant credibility among my peers and teachers.

As terrified and clueless as I was, my accent opened doors. I got many opportunities to "go to the ball and dance with the prince."

Since then, I've had several situations where I was in the right place at the right time. You might call this luck, but I call it the collision of my courage to go for it and the potential story *others were telling about me.*

Courage, I could control. Potential, I couldn't, because "people with British accents are clever" is a social construct—and one that gave me a massive advantage.

Thanks to this social construct, people in power could easily see my future capacity. When it comes to filling a role, I fit their idea of "how things should be done."

If I'd had a different accent, there's a good chance the social construct in place would've worked against me. I would have been seen as less clever, and my potential harder to recognize. This happens to brilliant people every day.

Knowing this, I teach leaders to recognize how much easier it is to apply potential stories to others when they look and sound like their experiences.

And I'm not just talking about accents here.

I worked in Ad Technology for years. It's easier for me to see the courage and potential in a bright, energetic young woman because once I was a bright, energetic young woman working in Ad Technology.

I'm biased. We're all biased. Leaders are responsible for owning their biases and cultivating diverse-thinking teams on purpose.

Finding it harder to recognize potential in others isn't a flaw in your leadership strategy unless you choose to intentionally ignore it. And I sincerely hope you don't.

Ready to implement this idea? I'll guide you through it.
Go to talesofpotential.com/discover

When it Comes to the Future, Everyone Is Guessing

If you're in the process of a role change, you've probably noticed that "the ability to embrace ambiguity" shows up on job postings. Quite often.

How would you know if you've got what the hiring manager is looking for in that department? What's an excellent example of someone embracing ambiguity?

Cinderella knows.

So, according to her stepmother, Cinderella was not up for a promotion to a better life. And never would be. Do your chores well, and you may well prevent your life from worsening—that was the message.

And this stay-where-you-are message was reinforced when the stepsisters shredded the homemade ball gown. In other words, there was no ambiguity at all in Cinderella's place in life.

But then the Fairy Godmother arrived. And with the wave of her magic wand, everything changed—which is also to say, she made all that soul-crushing certainty about Cinderella's dismal life possibilities disappear.

Hooray! And also, yikes.

You may have noticed in your own life that when you punch through the wall you've been banging your head against (metaphorically speaking, I hope), you get a massive adrenaline surge.

But after the fist-pumping and dancing subside, you find yourself completely disoriented. Like, holy crap, now what?

When we have breakthroughs, possibilities abound, yet "right answers" become elusive. That's why it's scary even when the change is good news, and you've worked hard towards this outcome. Some of us backtrack into the knowable past; the lack of options suddenly looks familiar and kind of cozy.

Change creates ambiguity, and nothing can change for the better without it.

The dramatic transformation from servant to princess that Cinderella went through—she couldn't have pulled that off without a willingness to embrace ambiguity. And if she were asked to share about times when that willingness led to excellent outcomes, she might say:

The royal ball was a rare opportunity for me to advance my life goals. I desperately wanted to be there. But I didn't have the means to get a gown and had no idea how to solve this problem. So I leaned on what I did have—a small but mighty team. We pieced one together, a seed of an idea and a tiny bit of material at a time. And we finished the gown production just in time for the big night.

Or:

When I arrived at the royal ball, I was aghast. It dawned on me that I'd only been rehearsing the dancing part of the evening. And no one, not even the Fairy Godmother who sponsored my attendance, had mentioned gatekeepers. I'd have to pass by them before I could get to the dance floor. All I knew then was that if I acted as panicked as I felt, I'd look out of place. So I channeled regality as best I could. My first steps out of the coach were shaky and awkward. But by the time I reached the guards, I'd learned to walk with a smile and my head held high. Much to my relief and delight, they let me through, no problem.

So now you see what kind of qualities modern hiring managers are looking for. Maybe you're brimming with confidence and remembering times you've accomplished something similar in times of uncertainty.

But if you aren't, don't lose heart. I have good news for you.

I've had a lot of experience shifting from certainty to ambiguity—both for myself and as a team leader. And I can tell you that when you don't know the "right" answer, you have the freedom to create a new future for yourself.

You can experiment and see what might work when you can't predict what will happen in any given situation.

When no one else knows what might happen, you have the space to make mistakes that teach you unforgettable lessons.

Choose to look at the future as an adventure, an experiment, a learning opportunity, and you, too, can do as Cinderella did: sweat over your close calls, cringe at your blatant mistakes, and laugh at it all later as you bring your hopes and dreams within reach.

You can make it through the gates of opportunity, even if your first steps are shaky and awkward.

Re-tell the tale of ambiguity.

I've lost count of the leaders who've told me they want "the person who's done it before" when they're looking to fill a vital role on their team. They're looking for a guarantee of results by repeating what the person did in the past.

I get it; they're looking for expertise and want to make a safe decision.

The same people also understand that their situation, current market dynamics, and the people involved differ. So although they won't necessarily say it out loud, these folks are also looking for someone who can embrace ambiguity. They want someone who considers both the recreate factor (duplicate the past) and the reinvent factor (create a new future).

So when you're talking to your team or hiring for a role, which priority are you messaging?

More importantly, do you know what you need?

It's worth noting that we tend to play it safe when ambiguity is high. And if ambiguity is high, then I'm guessing change is ahead.

So, don't you want to hire reinventors in any case?

And for the record, the stepsisters are recreators, while Cinderella is a reinventor.

People Don't Choose
Inauthenticity

∞

Cinderella has made it past the gates into the ballroom, and she's just started walking toward the dance floor. All eyes are on her, and folks are judging everything about her. It's an understandably scary situation.

What do we tend to do in situations like this?

We try to fit in. We try to be like everyone else. Very often, we try to be someone we're not.

That feels safer than being ourselves. As the thinking goes, if people judge our made-up persona, any judgment or rejection that comes our way won't be so personal.

Here's the problem. When we try to be someone we're not, other people get confused about what they're opting in to. Who you are and who you're presenting aren't the same thing. And people can tell in an instant.

Think about the last time you met someone and thought, "there's something about them that seems fake," or there was "something about them I just didn't like." You were picking up on their lack of authenticity.

So be polite, respectful, welcoming, and all the things you want to offer, but ultimately be yourself. Let people see you as you are so they can choose that person, not a slightly altered version of you.

And here's an idea to make being yourself easier next time you're risking rejection in an all-eyes-on-you situation.

Whisper to yourself, as the Fairy Godmother surely did to Cinderella when the coach door was closing:

"You are ready for anything that happens tonight. Don't worry about trying to be anyone else. Don't worry about what others are thinking. Just be as you are right now. For that is who you want people to choose. You."

Re-tell the tale of authenticity

I once got the most painful feedback. My manager said that others saw me as "political."

What I heard with this word "political" was manipulative and inauthentic. If you know me, you'll know that this is the last person I want to be. I was confused, too, since the only thing I was trying to do was make things happen.

The idea that people didn't like me crushed my spirit. The voice in my head was unkind. It took me a LONG time to realize how to solve the problem.

Why? Because I took the wrong lesson from the feedback my manager gave me (feedback I needed, by the way).

I heard, "I need to make them like me more," rather than "let them opt in to you just as you are."

Fortunately, I had a mentor at that same organization who said,

"Hey Joanna, we see how brilliant and confident you are with your team. We recognize how you empower them and bring out the best in them. We don't see that same person when you sit down with us. It's like you're trying to hide something from us. Can we have the same person you are with your team?"

When I heard this, a lightbulb went off in my head.

We all know what happens when you try to force someone to like you. It rarely ends well.

Let my mistake be your guide for choosing better.

(Leaders, I know that giving feedback and helping someone be all they can be is hard. Your best bet is to recognize who YOU want them to be and let them tell you who they think they can be.)

Ready to implement this idea? I'll guide you through it.
Go to talesofpotential.com/discover

The Dress Wasn't
About Being Beautiful

Finally! Cinderella has been seen and is about to get the job interview of her life.

You might be thinking, "Thank goodness for the spectacular dress! Cinderella had a lot of competition, and the Fairy Godmother made her so freaking beautiful."

But as I see it, the point of the magical, upgraded dress, shoes, and other bedazzlements was never solely for winning the prince. Cinderella being beautiful wasn't even the point of the makeover.

What was the point, then, you ask?

It was about giving Cinderella that "free upgrade swagger."

Allow me to explain.

Think about a time you got a surprise complimentary upgrade somewhere—the rental car check-in counter, swanky hotel, or hot new restaurant in town. I'll bet you instantly stood a bit taller. You owned whatever room you were in.

You felt grand. You believed in your awesomeness for at least a moment.

Imagine if you'd received this free upgrade on your way to a big interview or pitch meeting. How much would it have helped with your confidence? I know—a lot.

Now, back to Cinderella. Was the upgraded dress more stunning than the original? Yes, absolutely.

It was a dream of cascading satin silk in a shade of sky blue perfectly matched to bring out Cinderella's eyes. The frothy layers of crinoline beneath gave the skirt oomph and drama.

On top of that, she got perfectly-fitting gloves, a just-so-swoop to her updo, and those custom glass slippers. (No Fairy Godmother worth her salt would forget how much power and influence a pair of shoes can exert.)

But, again, making Cinderella more beautiful wasn't the point of the magic. The end goal was to help Cinderella recognize that she was amazing.

It's true that even without the upgrade, Cinderella already had the curiosity and bravery to step into the coach. But being bold in the ballroom would take a new level of courage. She needed to believe she could do it and that she was something special.

That's why the free upgrade—and the swagger that goes with it—mattered.

Cinderella needed to feel like she could own the room. Because walking into the room was just the first step in the "interview" process.

Ready to implement this idea? I'll guide you through it.
Go to talesofpotential.com/discover

Re-tell the tale of introductions.

Did you know that you give someone a gown every time you introduce them?

Let me paint you a picture. You're in a leadership meeting with your peers, discussing the best cross-functional team for a specific project. One of the roles needs to be filled by someone from your group. Let's call her Lauren.

You could say,

"I'm going to have Lauren lead this because she's great."

or,

"I'm going to have Lauren lead this because she has a unique perspective on the intersection of technology and storytelling, a perspective I think this team would find helpful."

By saying these things—

1. You've given Lauren immediate credibility.

2. You've helped the people in the room understand why Lauren is great.

3. You've made it easier for your peers to explain why they'll be working with Lauren to their team members.

4. Lauren will approach this project confidently and with clarity about why she's on the project.

The words, "Unique perspective on the intersection of technology and storytelling" = the dress.

By making it easier for others to opt in to Lauren, you've accelerated the potential for great things to happen.

And as a leader, you want to be an accelerator, right?

Ready to implement this idea? I'll guide you through it.
Go to talesofpotential.com/discover

Shortcuts Might Shortcut Opportunities (Why Magic Isn't Always The Answer)

No one wants to reach their goals slowly. If you can make things happen faster, why not?

Oh, but there is, in fact, an often overlooked harm in prioritizing speed: shortcuts might cause you to jump over better opportunities, opportunities you can't afford to miss.

The Fairy Godmother didn't magic Cinderella from her house to the top of the ballroom stairs for good reason. And if she had, Cinderella would have missed out on at least two crucial opportunities.

Missed Opportunity 1

You forget that the people in the ballroom weren't the only decision-makers. Team Royal Family Incorporated (TRF Inc.)

is not only the prince and parents. There's the entire organization making the court of TRF Inc. operate.

By having Cinderella pass by and probably (albeit briefly) interact with all the individuals who run TRF Inc., they're getting to opt in to a future with her.

Think about the last time your company added an executive to your organization. Didn't you want to know who they were and why the leadership team chose them? Even better, wouldn't you like to have had the opportunity to vet the candidates?

The more opportunities the team gets to opt in to new leaders, the faster the leader will integrate into the team and ultimately succeed.

Remember, the hiring manager is never the only decision-maker.

Missed Opportunity 2

Let's also not forget that the Fairy Godmother instantly transformed Cinderella from disheveled and weepy to glam and fabulous. Poof anyone from that state directly into the palace, and they'd have difficulty getting composed.

Not to mention, the slow carriage ride must have been a blast! Her team of supporters—the mice and goose—surrounded her, and they probably cheered her along the whole way there.

By giving Cinderella the experience of entering the palace grounds and allowing for time to watch, listen, and learn as she entered with the other guests, the Fairy Godmother ensured Cinderella had a moment to center herself.

So when she took her turn on the staircase, she could do so with confidence.

I find it so odd that we expect people to be their best selves when we throw them into unfamiliar situations. (I applaud today's recruiter, who's clearly taking on a more integrative role, gently preparing candidates to be their best selves when the moment comes.)

The steps along the way that seem tedious or mundane are more valuable than you might think. Fast-tracking your meet-and-greet with someone powerful, or any other "there" you're trying to reach, can come at a cost.

And besides, shouldn't we all enjoy a fantastic carriage ride before showtime? What's the rush, anyway?

Re-tell the tale of professional hacks.

We're inundated with headlines like "10 ways to…" or "This is how you do X." Clickbait headlines tell us that this one simple hack is the path to success all day long.

Shortcut-type advice often talks about the what, but it doesn't let the recipient experience the how. And while it might look like it helps people advance faster, there's always a cost.

While I'm a fan of periodically throwing people into the deep end, we need to ensure we're creating opportunities for our team members to practice expanding their awesomeness.

Follow these steps to ensure you're allowing your team to experience the how:

1. **Put them in the environment to practice**— even in the hybrid world of real-life and virtual; there's always an opportunity to make sure someone's not in a space for the first time. Practice builds confidence.

2. **Walk your stairs**—practice isn't just building a deck and a presentation outline. Get your team to run through ideas out loud. Have them say what they want to say to the other person before they have to say it out loud the first time.

3. **If they need a cheerleading section, create one**— I have a squad. I practice with them, and we're there to remind each other how amazing we are when we need it.

It's also worth noting that shortcut-thinking shows up in how companies deliver certain programming—and expect immediate results.

★ Go to this DEI training, and your biases will magically disappear.

★ Go to this Empower Women workshop, and you, a female team member, will come back empowered.

★ Take this leadership class, and you'll be able to lead.

★ Do these 10 things, and success will be yours.

But just because someone took a course doesn't mean the lesson stuck.

Just because someone's learned something new doesn't mean their underlying beliefs are now different.

Don't get me wrong; DEI, empowering women, and leadership classes are all brilliant ideas. Work/Life balance programs and time management courses also have value—except when they're window dressing. True transformation requires addressing the hard stuff beneath the surface.

And finally, note how hack culture is deceptively change-averse. It protects the status quo and promotes a "cheat code" way of life that ultimately benefits the existing power structure more than the individual.

So, be discerning with your professional hacks. If your goal is to take advantage of a power up, you're better off identifying what new skills you need and committing to learning over time. And allowing your team to do the same.

Ready to implement this idea? I'll guide you through it.
Go to talesofpotential.com/discover

If They Can't See You, They Can't Choose You

Every decision made about you is made in a room you're not in.

(The audience gasps every time I say this at a performance. So go ahead. Take a moment to let that sink in.)

If you aren't seen by the people who are in the room—if they don't know you want the opportunity—you can't be in the consideration set. The decision-makers can't choose you and your potential even if they want to.

Cinderella may not have known how to appeal to a prince looking for the perfect partner. But she knew something about being seen for the opportunity.

At this point in the story, Cinderella has made eye contact with the prince. She doesn't know what will happen next, but she knows this: getting invited into the room where critical decisions are made doesn't guarantee that someone will listen to you.

And now that their eyes had met, Cinderella wasted no time announcing her candidacy for the open position.

She held her head up high. She maintained the air of a Golden Globe nominee gracing the red carpet, quietly saying, "Hello, I'm here," with each deliberate step.

We're quick to associate kind, generous, and nice women like Cinderella with not having significant wants. Or at least being incredibly modest about demonstrating their wishes.

But make no mistake: Cinderella wanted to be talked about.

She wanted the prince to know what made her incredible—and for him to talk convincingly about her awesomeness to the king, queen, and whomever else with decision-making power.

She knew well that the decision about who'd be chosen for the opportunity to join Team Royal would be made in a room she wasn't in.

Whatever fear Cinderella may have had at that moment seems not to have been greater than her enthusiasm for the potential future job on her kingdom's leadership team.

So she took responsibility for the part of the process where she had some control.

She did not duck into the room through a side door. She stood alone at the top of the stairs. And she let herself be seen.

Re-tell the tale of visibility.

When presenting this idea that "every decision made about you is made in a room you're not in," this is what I say next:

"What they're saying is what you've taught them. So think about what you want to teach people about your potential."

And even this is true only if the room's occupants know they should be talking about you.

Cinderella made herself visible with the help of her team. But ultimately, SHE had to stand at the top of the stairs and enter the ballroom. It's quite the tale of courage.

Leaders, what are you doing to help your team get to the top of their staircase? And when they're up there, are they showing the courage of Cinderella?

You are the person in the "room they're not in." What story of potential are you teaching? Are you helping them be visible?

Ready to implement this idea? I'll guide you through it.
Go to talesofpotential.com/discover

Learn How To Waltz Before You Need to Know How to Waltz

People talk about luck all the time. They usually mention the word in an, "if only I were lucky, then…" context.

For luck to work out the way most people imagine it, you must be ready for the opportunity when it presents itself.

For example, if someone wants to dance with a prince, they need to know how to dance before showing up for the dance.

Sounds ridiculously simple, right?

Cinderella's story would have come to a grinding halt had she not known how to dance when the prince reached out his hand. (I'm cringing a little imagining the disaster that could have played out.)

Cinderella needed to know how to dance to collaborate with the prince.

Cinderella needed to know how to dance so she could be confident when he asked.

I have no idea how she taught herself to dance, but she did her part in preparing for luck to strike. And when luck arrived, she was a skilled dancer for the prince and herself.

What dance do you need to learn to be ready for your lucky moment when you get asked?

Re-tell the tale of preparation.

When was the last time someone on your team asked for a promotion or a raise, and you said, "You're not ready" or "Maybe next time"?

I'm guessing they responded with, "But I did everything you said I should do to get a promotion. I don't understand."

I get that you're not always the person who's the final or only decision-maker when it comes to promotions. That conversation is a book in itself.

Here's what I'd like you to think about.

First, do you have a Cinderella on your team who's taught themselves something without you noticing?

The fairy tale Cinderella learned how to dance, yet we had NO idea until the prince grasped her hand. And wow, did she deliver! The quiet person on the team has more skills and experiences than what's just in their job description; find out what they are. You might find a hidden talent that wows you.

Second, are you transparent with your team about what others need to believe about them?

People are promoted because of their ability to do things in the future, justified by what they've done in the past.

So don't just focus on past results in your conversations. Help them see that the future story (their potential) matters, too.

Ready to implement this idea? I'll guide you through it.
Go to talesofpotential.com/discover

Just Because You're Part of a Team Does Not Mean You'll Be Seen

———— ∞ ————

Have you ever wondered why the stepmother and stepsisters never seemed to see Cinderella while they were in the ballroom? How (uncharacteristically, I may add) did they not intervene and bring the interlude with the prince to an end?

It's because they, like many people, had potential blindness.

They could never see Cinderella's true potential outside her role as an indentured servant, which meant she was, in turn, invisible to them when she wasn't in that role. This potential blindness isn't unique to fairy tales; it happens in real life, too.

To help illustrate this point, let's jump out of the human context for a moment.

Can you imagine four dimensions? Can you see what four dimensions look like?

No? I can't, either. But stay with me. Let's do an experiment together.

Take a piece of paper and draw two circles. One inside the other. Something like this.

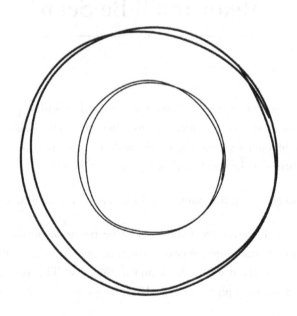

Simple right?

Now, if I asked you to move the smaller circle to be outside the larger circle, could you do it without breaking the larger circle?

In two dimensions, you can't.

In three dimensions, you can. Change the lines on the paper and turn them into a string, shifting a two-dimensional image into a three-dimensional object. Now you can lift the inner circle up and out of your donut shape; voila, you have two circles.

Ok. You can "see" two and three dimensions by imagining them.

Now take those two pieces of string and loop them together like hoops. You currently have two connected circles in three dimensions. Like the first exercise, can you separate the circles without cutting the string?

In three dimensions, you can't.

In four dimensions, you can.

Can you see it? No, neither can I. But mathematically, it's possible.

We're both blind to the potential of the fourth dimension even though we know that the fourth dimension exists.

No magic was needed to keep the stepmother and stepsisters from seeing Cinderella at the palace, exhibiting the kind of potential they'd never associate with her. As in the fourth dimension, they couldn't see something they didn't recognize.

The question then becomes, where else might we be blind?

Re-tell the tale of possibility.

Our capacity to see someone's potential is affected by our experiences, expectations, and levels of assumed alike-ness.

Beware that when it comes to potential, "If I can't see it, it must not be there" is often dangerously untrue.

Ready to implement this idea? I'll guide you through it.
Go to talesofpotential.com/discover

The Prince (Mostly) Showed Modern Leadership Qualities

As I described in Part 1 of this book, everyone needs someone—usually lots of someones—for their ambitions to manifest. Nobody does it alone.

And even though I said *nobody*, you may still think powerful people like the prince are an exception.

Well, let me tell you something. This prince did not think that was the case.

I know, I know, he seems vain. But the prince *did* turn down every prospective union his parents had proposed.

Some of the women had to have been gorgeous. Some of the money or resources advantages on the table had to have been significant. And the pressure to conform to customs alone must have been tremendous.

Yet his answer was always, "No, thanks."

Why did the prince persist? Because the prince had unique ambitions. And he needed a partner to complement his particular skills and experiences.

He understood that diversified thinking combined to solve problems in the future was key to solving problems for everyone. And isn't that what a future king needs in the role of the queen?

His actions suggest he sought a vibrant partner connected to the community and the land he was entrusted with governing. He could imagine overseeing a thriving kingdom that wasn't reliant on territory grabbing, resource control, and heirs produced with wealthier neighbors.

Here are three more overlooked qualities that, in my opinion, make the prince awesome.

1. **He was willing to go against his boss** (yes, that would be his parents), and he was pretty persuasive.

   Showing resistance within a hierarchical power dynamic is courageous in and of itself. But this prince took things further and got his parents to sign off on his partner candidate search plan. A wide net, in-kingdom search, the likes of which had never been attempted before. And he convinced his bosses without manipulation.

   It's too bad we don't get a better glimpse into the prince's thinking because his persuasion skills are top-notch, and his example is worth learning from.

2. He saw potential in Cinderella, not just her qualifications.

It wasn't hard for the prince to recognize that Cinderella could both stand out and connect with the audience—the crowd's reaction to her presence at the ball was confirmation enough. The humility, grace, and quiet intensity she exuded in their more private moments were attractive qualities, too.

Even better, he could imagine how she'd bring his vision to life and make it *theirs*, not just follow a script previous kings and queens had laid out for them. He recognized that Cinderella was very much a qualified candidate for future shenanigans.

And so, when the prince later saw her in an everyday state of soot-covered rags and grimy knees, it didn't matter. Nothing about her appearance and "true identity" took away from the potential he'd already seen in her.

3. He leveraged his power when needed.

The prince didn't throw tantrums, triangulate, or pull any other dirty power moves at any stage of the partner-search process. But he did have power, and he leveraged it when called for.

After all, he didn't go door-to-door hand-delivering the invitations to the ball. He didn't direct the valet for the coaches. He didn't keep a watchful eye on the servers passing drinks and appetizers. Heck, when it comes to the ball, he might not have done anything but pick the date and approve the guest list.

As an executive, it's appropriate to concentrate one's energy on building a team and then entrusting the team members to do their jobs superbly.

And in case you hadn't noticed, instead of micromanaging the ball, the prince was laser-focused on the one job only he could do: to find, choose, and court the top candidate for his leadership team.

Let's take this story and fast-forward it to the present time. Can you see the prince as an executive? And if so, wouldn't you say he has the skills and qualities we look for in a modern-day leader? I sure would.

(And honestly, let's toss all the gender stereotypes out the window. Prince, princess, Cinderella, or Cinderfella—I hope you can see every person in every possible role, including the part of Fairy Godmother.)

Re-tell the tale of executive profiles.

You weren't expecting that, were you? Cinderella's story isn't the only tale of potential we've heard wrong.

I hope you see that the prince's profile is fantastic for current leaders of all genders: someone with a vision, who negotiates well, who trusts their team and works with focus, and who also sees potential in a candidate beyond the obvious.

The prince was telling the tale of *his* potential. As a leader, how are you telling yours?

Ready to implement this idea? I'll guide you through it.
Go to talesofpotential.com/discover

Why a Glass Slipper is Better Than a Resume

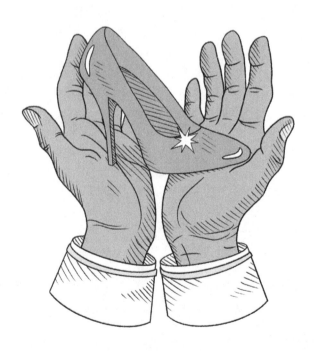

Let's talk about the glass slippers, shall we? They were the stars of the climactic staircase scene and the key to the prince tracking down the enchanting mystery woman he'd danced with.

Have you ever wondered why the shoes were the only bit of magic that didn't disappear after midnight? It was no accident. I'd argue that it was the most intentional piece of the Fairy Godmother's magic.

Picture yourself, if you will, auditioning.

Whether that audition is a job interview, a pitch meeting for a contract, or something else, we generally focus on two things:

1. Landing the invitation to become a finalist. (Usually by parading all of our qualifications in front of the decision-makers and gatekeepers).

2. Being smooth and on point. (So we look like we belong in the room while we have face time).

We give those two things 99% of our attention and use the remaining 1% to follow up.

Then we pray.

We pray the decision-makers aren't distracted by all the other options at their fingertips. We pray that when they need to explain to their bosses and teams why they chose YOU, they have all the language and details to describe "why you."

That's right. Most of us rely on hopes, prayers, and crossed fingers to close the gap between dreaming and living the dream.

Not the Fairy Godmother and Cinderella, though.

Let's take a moment to bring the fairy tale and real worlds together. You'll see how the shoe—not crossed fingers, hopes, and prayers—kept helping the prince remember Cinderella and make the best decision for his future.

★ At about 12:15 am, our prince realized that chasing wouldn't get him his girl that night. He was probably quite perplexed. The night, however, was still young. I imagine he went back into the ballroom to say hello to some of his friends. Was there another qualified candidate still in the room? Yes, a good two hundred of them. Did the shoe remind him that he'd already chosen "the one"? Also yes. The shoe was a differentiator.

★ Let's roll forward to the following day. Remember how the prince held that lone shoe, yearning to know more about its owner and imagining the beautiful future he could create with her? And how he landed on the brilliant idea to search for the person whose foot perfectly fit into it? The shoe catalyzed the reunion plan.

★ Now the prince is all, "I gotta find that girl!" But you'll remember his parents had been nagging him the day before that he needed to find a partner in life or they would choose one for him. This was the point of having the ball in the first place. So before our young Prince heads out to track her down, he needs to update his boss (his parents) and his management team (his peers and staff) that he'd found "the one".

What did he have to help them see her potential to be perfect? You guessed it, a shoe. The shoe was a marketing tool to help him sell the idea to his parents. (Yes, it is odd that teeny tiny feet signify awesomeness. But do remember we're in a fairy tale.)

For all that Cinderella got right at the ball, she couldn't have secured the role she was after without something the prince to remember her by.

Of course, the prince could have proposed to Cinderella on the spot, preferably by 11:55 p.m. But he didn't. We must remember that in real life, as in fairy tale land, people make significant decisions in a similar way, taking time to reflect even if they were smitten at the first meeting.

There's a whole industry dedicated to creating "shoes" to help you remember a product and company. Those branded company gifts—hoodies, coffee mugs, mini-chargers and such—aim to capture your good feeling about their brand in physical form.

They help brands be remembered. They also allow you to track them down, whether that tracking happens right away or in the future. They work.

Oddly enough, few people use this tactic when trying to be remembered by another person. So if you do, you, my friend, will easily stand out.

You deserve to get your ambitions over the chasm between idea and reality. So go ahead and create a shoe. And watch what happens when you give people something to remember you by.

Re-tell the tale of resumes.

Important decisions get made with a bit of reflection, even when the decision-maker is 100% sure of their final choice during the meeting. The person opting in to you needs to both remember you AND be able to explain "why you" to someone else.

Knowing that, will you continue to let their memory and resume do all the work for you?

I know all of you hiring managers think you need a candidate's resume. But think about it for a second. What kind of smartphone do you own? Did you buy it because of its detailed and fabulous user manual? No, I didn't, either.

Research shows that a presentation's "visual" and "vocal" elements heavily influence how an audience responds to it. What's written only represents 7% of why someone likes your total presentation package.

Wouldn't it be easier for others to remember and recognize who we are—and how we can help solve problems in the future— if we brought a visual or physical element to the conversation about potential?

You know it would, just as it did for Cinderella.

So what could the visual look like in a modern working world?

One of my clients, Shannon, had a non-linear career path. She'd gone from consulting, to law, to CFO, and her path (and her genius) was confusing to people.

So we created a timeline graphic that wove the "how I got here" into something that made sense. It ultimately became a differentiator for Shannon when she faced an interview process with 19 other candidates.

Shannon Career Timeline

The idea goes beyond the job search. Lisa Van Dusen, an executive at SV2 (a Silicon Valley Venture Fund), unapologetically shares her stunning watercolors. In doing so, she messages to her team, customers, and network that she is as much an artist as a business-savvy executive. Through her art, you learn WHO she is; through her business acumen, you can see the IMPACT she can make.

I keep a plain notepad by my desk when I offer virtual sessions. I use it to whip up a quick Venn diagram of potential when I'm working with someone. When I do, their perspective (as well as the rest of the audience's) shifts from "this could work" to "I see this working."

Look, here's mine. Does it tell you a story about how I think?

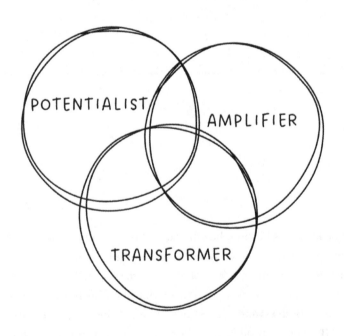

Imagine I ripped it out of the notepad and handed it to you. Would it help you remember who I am?

Visuals help tell a story.

Give some thought to how you'll offer the person holding the key to your dreams something juicy to remember you by, something that will remind them of your uniqueness. The slipper (or scribbles on a torn piece of paper) might be the difference between a near miss and a dream come true.

PS. I think job descriptions are equally antiquated. Let's sort them out, too, shall we?

Ready to implement this idea? I'll guide you through it.
Go to talesofpotential.com/discover

Sometimes Done is Better Than Perfect

———— ∞ ————

Do you remember our earlier lesson about rule-breaking? Let me remind you just in case: on your way to making dreams come true, even a bona fide rule-following type of person must take on the task of turning nos into yesses.

Now, there's something else about breaking rules that I need to mention. There comes a time when saying yes to rules isn't an option.

That time came for Cinderella when the shoe fell off.

Until then, Cinderella had been a "good and perfect" person and teammate. It didn't matter how irrational the ask—from the stepmother, stepsisters, or the Fairy Godmother—she did what she was told and did it to the best of her abilities.

Let's pause on the palace steps and think for a moment about what was happening in Cinderella's brain. She had a choice.

Option A:
Do what I'm told and make a clean exit.

That means to grab the shoe, run like heck, and hope I don't get caught in the process. The Fairy Godmother said the rules were "get out before midnight," and I cannot fail her.

Option B:
Ditch the shoe and hope no one gets mad.

That means leaving the shoe as getting out of here is more strategically important. I'm sure the Fairy Godmother will be a bit annoyed, but I'm a bright girl, and we can come up with a solution to resolve this tomorrow.

Option C:
Strategy time.

If I leave the shoe, maybe, just maybe, it could be a creative tool for getting back in here tomorrow. And getting back here gives me another opportunity for the prince and crew to pursue a future with me. Plus, as the future queen of fairy tale land, I'll have the resources at my disposal to be generous and kind to the Fairy Godmother.

I say she chose Option C. Option B would have sufficed, but it was crucial that she not choose Option A. Why?

Because the fairy tale land needed a leader with the confidence to make hard decisions. Decisions whose rationale might not be immediately obvious (losing a shoe) or don't jive with what others say they should do (following the rules).

Do you remember the more modern Cinderella story? Tess McGill was Cinderella, Katherine Parker was the stepmother, Jack Trainer was the prince, and the royal ball, in this scenario, was a job. The fairy tale movie was called *Working Girl*.

At a pivotal moment in the movie, we find her squished into an elevator with her prince and the potential for a job. She says, "You can bend the rules plenty once you get to the top, but not while you're trying to get there. And if you're someone like me, you can't get there without bending the rules."

Tess got the job, and not because of her rule-following perfection or even her idea. She got the job because she showed the decision-maker, Oren Trask, the potential in her ability to think, and he, in turn, asked her to join her team. (I'll also add that she had visual tools to help her along the way.)

Whatever her inclinations may have been, Cinderella wisely chose not to retrieve the shoe. She took ownership of breaking the rules when necessary. She grasped what it means to prioritize good enough for now over perfect.

You already know how to be strategic. Believe in your decision-making, and don't just follow someone else's rules.

Re-tell the tale of perfection.

We often underestimate the risk of going for perfect and overestimate the risk of stopping at "done." And that can cost the mission. Both as leaders and individuals, we must be willing to walk that tightrope between perfect and future-focused.

We're taught at a young age to be perfect and get an A on all the tests because that's how one joins the winning team. Our education and entertainment messages are both "you've failed if you aren't perfect."

But perfect is impossible, and as a team leader, you're not looking for people who just do precisely what they are told. You want them to think, assess, and act in the best interests of the future.

You're going to have to help people unlearn the idea of perfect. Help them learn how to be like Cinderella and find out that sometimes done is better than perfect, and the only way to develop discernment is by getting practice.

Ready to implement this idea? I'll guide you through it.
Go to talesofpotential.com/discover

The Level-Up Happens When YOU Make It Happen

A surprise obstacle might get thrown your way even if you do everything right.

You know this to be true from every adventure movie you've ever seen: when the finish line is firmly in sight, you'd better watch out for the villainous plot twist.

And Cinderella's adventure was no exception, was it? Her stepmother locked her up in the attic when the attendants with the glass slipper arrived.

Here are a few things we can learn from these critical final scenes of the fairy tale, from cinders to celebrations.

1. Sometimes the boss makes mistakes.

For all her strategy and intentionality, it seems the Fairy Godmother had no idea the stepmother was going to try to stop Cinderella so close to the finish of the story. Locking her up in that attic room just as the prince arrived for the shoe-try-on experiment was unconscionable. Cinderella didn't wait for the Fairy Godmother to reappear and fix the problem, though: she had her squad to support her, and she took matters into her own hands.

2. If you want to be empowered to make bold strategic moves, then make some bold strategic moves.

You may have someone in your life who's on the sidelines, watching, tweaking things as needed, or stepping in and making some magic happen as the Fairy Godmother did for Cinderella. As you level up, show your capacity to navigate complexity without this person. It's the final step in the shift from them empowering you to you being empowered all by yourself.

Leaders and mentors, let's take a moment to unpack this part of the story through the Fairy Godmother's lens.

I suspect she knew she'd need to let Cinderella move on and create a future for herself. This oops moment at her stepmother's house undoubtedly helped the Fairy Godmother see that Cinderella was ready to brave the future all by herself.

As a Fairy Godmother myself, my stance is that I'll always be there for my Cinderellas, and I'll always be curious about what they're doing. But there comes a time when I no longer need to tweak things behind the scenes. When this time comes, it's always a bittersweet moment. That you are no longer needed hurts a little.

But I also know it means they have all the confidence, tools, and a great squad—their equivalent of Cinderella's prince and his family—to collaborate with them. Getting to this point is always what I am hoping for.

In those final moments, Cinderella didn't need to tell the Fairy Godmother she was ready; she acted like she was. She showed the world how empowered she was to build her future.

Re-tell the tale of who you can be.

Sometimes you need to convince your best advocates that you can do the new thing before they let you be the new thing. And proving it is going to take action.

I know it may feel like your boss, your advocate, your champion is holding you back. It just might be that they're so close to the story of who you are that they, too, can't let go of the story of who you can be. Unlike the stepmother, they're not villains. They're not out to get you on purpose.

The sooner you start "acting as if" rather than waiting for permission, the sooner others will see you that way too.

Like Cinderella, there's a moment you'll need to step forward and be the person you need to be next. Then your boss, like Cinderella's Fairy Godmother, can applaud and cheer behind the scenes as you step into your new future.

Ready to implement this idea? I'll guide you through it.
Go to talesofpotential.com/discover

There is Power
in Exiting Gracefully

As Cinderella leaves her home for the palace and a new life, I want to share my thoughts on first and last impressions.

Even if the situation you're leaving is despicable, you don't need to go out in a blaze of glory. There's power in exiting gracefully. Cinderella made a point of exercising this kind of grace.

Was the stepmother a toxic boss? Yes.

Did Cinderella owe her family any grace or kindness? Nope.

Fairy tale or modern world, I don't think any of us would blink if Cinderella had asked her husband-to-be to burn the place down. At the very least, she could have had the family arrested for abuse and goodness knows what else.

But there she stood, on the steps of the only home she'd known, and she forgave. The last impression she left with her stepfamily was love and compassion. (If you're wondering how she pulled this off, go back and read *Take a Walk in Their Shoes Instead* in Part 1.)

Forgiving wasn't a powerful move just because it was aspirationally good and moral. It was a powerful move because the first impression Cinderella gave her new family was grace. Never forget that the end of something is the beginning of something else.

Own your last impression; it's as critical as your first. Often it's one and the same.

We've reached the end of Part 2 and exploring The Near You, the land of opportunity seizing. At this transition, I want you to, once again, review the Potential Tales and make notes about what you've learned.

And if you do nothing else, my dear reader, take a beat to consider this.

What do you want people to remember you for?

PART 3

———— ∞ ————

The Future
You +
Cinderella

In Part 2, we watched as Cinderella's narrative transformed yet again.

At the start, it was this. "The slightly pathetic girl was rescued by a Fairy Godmother and chosen by a prince. All thanks to her dazzling beauty."

And it transformed into this. "The curious ingenue participated in the Fairy Godmother's magic with courage, wit, and grace. And the prince (wisely) pursued her for the open leadership role on TRF Inc."

I shared how seizing opportunities (and creating opportunities for others) involves preparing for luck with skill-building, making potential visible to others, and engaging a reinventor's mindset toward navigating ambiguity.

I also made a case for bringing a "shoe" to the decision-making room to help others remember your awesomeness.

And now, we're at the happy conclusion of the adventure. The conclusion as we know it, anyhow.

I've always wondered what happened after the sentence, "And they all lived happily ever after." Haven't you?

Assuming that everything was perfect from the moment when the prince proposed seems a bit ridiculous. And yet, that assumption plays out in our real lives.

We imagine that everything will be perfect when we get the promotion. We believe our dream job will have us bouncing out of bed every morning, ready to take on the day.

We think that the person we just hired will solve all our problems. We believe our new manager will be the kind of leader we need them to be every day.

It's all fairy tale thinking. Real life is just not like that.

So, the core question for Part 3, The Future You, is this:

How do you navigate an ambiguous future when you need to balance possibility and reality?

Shall we all look into the future with our heroine Cinderella? And see what she can teach us as we try to write our very own "and they all lived happily ever after" career narrative?

And They All Lived
Happily Ever After

As the reframed tale unfolded, you may have noticed that I became *your* Fairy Godmother. That's right; I've been working magic to get you to this part of the journey, where you own the story you want to live in.

Here in Part 3, I don't have a Potential Tale to re-tell. That's because your role has shifted. Instead of me reframing the past, you're going to do the work of reframing your future.

Take heart if you don't feel ready to go it alone. I'm still here for you. But our remaining time together is short, and it's important to me that you can do this reframing work with confidence.

So first things first, we must unpack what the heck happily ever after is.

I know that you are not working your buns off just to land in some hazy dreamland that's hopefully good for you. You need a concrete example of how one step truly leads to another so you can be confident that what's on the other side is something you want.

Let me help with that. Here's my Fairy Godmother's view on how life post-wedding played out for Cinderella.

We know Cinderella puts effort into naming goals. She also describes whatever obstacles she's facing with great precision to anyone who offers help. And she readily accepts the magic offered.

She likely stayed that course, whether the goal was learning to speak a new language, traveling to a faraway land, or doing a major reorganization, so the voices of marginalized members in her kingdom are elevated.

We know that generosity is her core value. Long before becoming a member of the royal family, she offered her gift of a strong work ethic, resourcefulness, kindness, and the benefit of the doubt to everyone in her sphere.

By adding virtually every human in the kingdom to her sphere of influence, she no doubt found ways to spread generosity on a grander scale than before.

We know she lets herself be seen in critical moments and understands risk-taking. Candidates for various leadership roles must have sought her for counsel and support, especially the unlikely (but actually perfect) ones. I imagine her entering rooms where decisions are being made on behalf of these unlikely candidates, enticing people to listen to her fresh ideas and winning them over.

And, of course, we know that **she invests in her squad**, which grew from mice and birds.

Now that the squad includes the prince and the best and brightest of the palace staff, she must have carried out many glorious shenanigans with them and helped to manifest each other's ambitions, ambitions of every shape and form.

I want you to notice something here: these scenarios are all rooted in who Cinderella was—and the winning mindset she'd adopted and acted on—before she met the prince at the ball.

Her Future You was an extension of The Near You, which had evolved from The Now You.

Yes, the royal ball was a transformative experience, and joining Team Royal was a culmination of her ambition. But it was also just a step on the adventure that Cinderella had already set in motion.

Happily ever after is anything but a hazy dreamland. It means, "and on and on the fabulous adventure continued."

And the same is true for you.

That version of you living a glorious future? That person is alive inside who you are already. Cinderella had what it took to create her happily ever after, and you have what it takes, too.

Your happily ever after is unfolding at this very moment. You can write your Future You story into existence right from where you are.

Your Happily Ever After
Can Change Over Time

As we just saw, Cinderella didn't just ride off into the sunset after the wedding; she started a new adventure.

At this point in the story, that probably wasn't so surprising to learn. You know Cinderella had to make a whole new plan for herself, right?

While we're still on the topic of happily ever after, there's one last point I want to make.

Happily ever after isn't a destination at the end of a prescribed path.

That's as true for fairy tales as for career ambitions.

We do this silly thing of asking children what they want to be when they grow up. We even kind of expect them to follow their answers as they become adults! But I rarely meet someone who knows what they want to be.

And those people who say they always knew? Stuff and nonsense. Who they are now and who they thought they would be at the beginning of their "growing up" is nearly always different.

That's because happily ever after is dynamic. It changes as you learn and grow.

The part in fairy tales where you hear that three-word phrase seems like the end of the story, but in truth, it's still in the middle. You know that more goes on; you're just never told what.

Like Cinderella's dream come true story, your career can be an ever-evolving adventure. Not only do you not need to know "what you want" to get moving, but your happily ever after can and will change.

And also, like Cinderella, your ambitions are yours to design and define. What's right for you might not be suitable for someone else.

Care only about what's right for you.

You Want to Be Chosen
for Who You Are

I want to close Part 3 with some thoughts on authenticity: why it matters, what makes it hard, how it connects to your potential, and how it helps your ambition come to life.

Authentic, in my book, means putting yourself out there just the way you are—and having the confidence to allow others to choose you based on who you are right now.

You've already learned how being clear about yourself and equally clear about what you want to be known for leads to great things. And how, when you do that, it's pretty awesome for the people trying to choose you, too.

But I know that a teeny problem called fear gets in the way of this idea of authenticity spreading.

Just kidding! Fear is not a teeny problem at all. And the only way we can see this problem clearly is by naming what fear is like in action and describing what "inauthentic" looks like.

Luckily, we have a clear example of inauthenticity in the stepmother. Who she is in her day-to-day life is spectacularly different from the woman she becomes when the prince is at her doorstep. She's afraid to be seen as she is, so she hides it under a more pleasant veneer.

Think about any leader you'd define as authentic, and you'll notice they seem to be clear about who they are, offer it for consideration with confidence and let others choose them. Like Cinderella's, theirs is a fundamentally generous act.

Is reading that motivating? Yes. But so far, authenticity is still easier said than done. Why? Because the most important person you need to be authentic with is yourself.

I'll confess that even as a Modern Fairy Godmother, I struggle with this far too often.

I want everyone to choose me.
I want everyone to like me.

So I try to be everything to everyone. Not very authentic.

And then there's that "every decision made about you and your opportunities is made in a room you're not in" statement that applies to the decisions I make in my head.

You're not good enough.
Why would they want me?

While I know I'm spectacular at what I do, even I have conversations with myself and fight to have the courage to be authentic.

As a Modern Fairy Godmother, I work with all genders. I work with all nationalities. I work with anyone who wants help figuring out what they want to offer the world and how to help others opt in to them.

When most people hear Modern Fairy Godmother, the stories in their heads include old ladies, silliness, sequins, and feminine things. And I doubt they'd put Fairy Godmother in the professional bucket.

And yet, this is who I am.

I am a little silly. I like to laugh, and I talk nonstop about magic and transformations.

I dream about the day I can stand on stage unironically in a sequin ball gown with a wand, speaking about the future of work and how it could be so much better with a bit of transformation.

I also bring data and charts to my conversations. The tools I provide are both strategically impactful and tactically easy to use. I am both science and mystery.

I'll admit I considered writing this book under a masculine name. Why tell anyone I'm a woman if doing so would make it harder for half the population to opt into my ideas?

But now, I'm more convinced than ever that my ambition needs me to be authentic to manifest. It can't come to life any other way.

So throughout this book, I've presented these modern and future-focused ideas with equal parts magic and reason. I'm trying hard to be just as I am—like Cinderella was—and I think you should, too.

Your ambition, the Future You, needs *you* to be authentic to manifest. It can't come to life any other way.

I'm choosing you for who you are and not what you think you should be.

Here's a toast to meeting the Future You, living out your unique happily ever after in all your glory with your team in tow, sometime very soon.

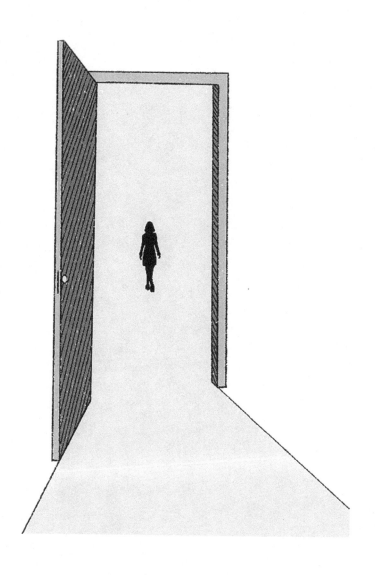

In Closing

Making Magic in the Real World

In Closing: Making Magic in the Real World

You and I aren't living in a fairy tale land. But I hope you've learned some lessons from our dear friend Cinderella's re-framed fairy tale. I hope she's got you thinking about how to rethink your story—and jumpstart the future of your dreams, no matter what setbacks you've suffered.

Before I go, I have a little more magic to sprinkle over your mind to get your future-thinking juices flowing.

Are you ready for it? Here we go.

What you want to be wanted for = what you are wanted for.

My vision is for this—what I call the Opt In Equation—to be your new career "normal." This equation can apply to all your evolutionary stages.

You've seen the examples. I know you've got this.

And as you go on this journey, please do not forget your role in making this equation true for other people.

Why?

Because every day, someone is chosen because of a story in someone else's head. It's a story that says, "They'll be performing and fitting into the team well!" and it pops up just like that.

Meanwhile, every day, someone else who has equal (if not greater) potential is not being chosen simply because lots of decision-makers can't conjure up a good future story about them.

There's a perception problem. It's widespread, and it reinforces a terrible status quo.

No matter your ambition, I know upholding the status quo isn't part of the picture. So I'd like to show you how you can be a magic-maker who shapes the world through what you opt in to.

10 Reasons Why Cinderella is a Great Candidate for the C-suite

In case it didn't stick, here's the Opt In Equation again:

**What you want to be wanted for =
what you are wanted for.**

As we just discussed, we tend to tell stories about people based on our perceptions. And if qualities like good at cleaning, a bit pathetic, needs to be rescued, has a lovely personality, etc. is what you see in Cinderella—which is true for most people who haven't read this book yet—you miss a lot of other things that are equally true about her.

Based only on their current title and the information we get from their resume, we can't help but underestimate people's potential.

And so, we count people, even ourselves, out of opportunities at which they (or we) could excel.

⭐ Exercise

You are on a company's board and need to find a new CEO. While the one you have was brilliant and had a vision for the product, you now need someone who can take this team to the next level.

They need to have that unicorn set of skills that balance humility with ambition, taking bold risks with understanding how to assess risks, and taking the lead while creating space for others to carve their path.

It's a critically important hire that will make or break the company. Their impact on customers and the team will be huge. You need to choose the right person for their future.

Ok. You have two candidates before you. They meet the qualifications you've sent out as part of the job description.

Candidate A went to the right schools, knows all the right people, comes with stellar references, and can be a bit high maintenance sometimes, but that's probably just a sign of their passion and drive.

They showed up on time, were full of personality, and proved they were prepared to do anything to get the job.

Candidate B graduated but not from a top-tier school and knows no one. Their one reference, unfortunately, has nothing noteworthy to say.

Even so, you've seen how much the people on this candidate's current team love being on their team. This person strikes you as being lovely.

Some details to note: they were late. And you're worried they lack confidence as they were a little quiet and had to leave quickly at the end for another appointment.

What story are you telling yourself about these two people?

I know it's a bit dramatic, but Candidate A was one of the stepsisters, Candidate B was Cinderella, and you, in this story, were the prince.

Lesson—don't assume the rules are cut and dry.

Now let's make sure you've understood Cinderella's story, that you've addressed the potential bias you know you probably have.

Have a good look at all that Cinderella made happen without a title. It's impressive. Without a preconceived story based on a title or credentials in your head, wouldn't you choose someone like her to lead your organization? Or would you still limit her to a cleaning role?

Consider what roles you would go for in real life—or support others in pursuing—if you could let go of the old story and trust the potential in you and them.

We've reviewed the prince's qualities as a modern-day leader. You know I wouldn't leave out a review of Cinderella's stellar leadership skills, right?

There are ten reasons why I think Cinderella would make a great CEO. Here they are.

1. **She can create things with extremely limited resources.** In some versions of the story, the stepmother sold off the family's possessions. Poor Papa was dead, and the family had no income. And yet, Cinderella figured out how to a) keep the house neat as a pin and b) keep dinner on the table.

2. **She entices her team to collaborate.** The mice and birds were genuinely happy to do things with and for Cinderella. It wasn't about pay. Now, if you haven't already noticed, getting others to do things is freaking hard. That's why managers are equipped with an arsenal of sticks and carrots: your access to future opportunities, your ability to get a good reference, your paychecks, how big they are, and whether or not you'll keep getting them. And yet, Cinderella fostered team collaboration and got sh*t done through intrinsic motivation. This is a very big deal.

3. **She's really good with difficult and demanding customers.** Hi, the stepsisters.

4. **She can handle a tyrannical boss.** Hi, the stepmother.

5. **She's 100% authentic.** She doesn't waver on or apologize for who she is and what she's about.

6. **She's clear about what she wants**. As you'll recall, she centered her life around the goal of spreading kindness and generosity. And she made decisions that supported her long game (turning her everyday life into a platform for her core

147

values rather than hatching the quickest escape) and the immediate game (quickly scraping together whatever bits and bobs she could in order to hand sew a dress for the ball).

7. **She's excellent at seizing opportunities when they present themselves.** Remember what distraught Cinderella did when the Fairy Godmother showed up? She delivered a concise speech about her goal (dance with the prince) and the roadblock she was facing (dress, gone). She didn't shrink or snark about her stepsisters. Her focused response proves that "every crisis is an opportunity" was very much Cinderella's mindset—before the Fairy Godmother appeared to work her magic.

8. **She knew how to dance, literally and figuratively.** She waltzed through a ton of I-don't-know-what-I'm-supposed-to-do situations just to get on the dance floor. And once there, she claimed the spotlight. You know that the best leaders don't wait around for correct answers to appear or feign modesty in high-stakes moments. Well, neither did Cinderella.

9. **She understood how to deal with deadlines.** Try as we may, we can't always flawlessly execute a plan. And the next-best options can all be high-risk. The shoe falling off situation tested Cinderella's capacity for walking this tightrope. Yes, her exit was a tad behind schedule, but she decisively left the slipper on the staircase and made the midnight deadline. Mission saved.

10. **She can close a deal, even without a title.** Did the prince need the reassurance of a fancy title to take a

chance on Cinderella? No, he did not. When you consider the importance of reviews and credentials in hiring or purchasing choices—what value other people assign to this person or thing you're considering—it's easier to appreciate the magnitude of Cinderella's achievement.

I'm not going to go through this exhaustive list with the step-sisters, but I'm sure you can guess how they'd react in these exact situations.

So who do you want to hire now?

Ready to implement this idea? I'll guide you through it.
Go to talesofpotential.com/discover

You Can Be a
Fairy Godmother

When I speak, the audience looks at the person on stage or in the hot seat receiving a story transformation, and their eyes say, "It must be nice...if only *I* had a Fairy Godmother like them."

Much as I'd love to, I can't be everywhere and magic everyone.

So, if we never have the pleasure of meeting in person, please remember this: everyone you *do* meet could be your Fairy Godmother. Be open to this possibility, approach people as though they have magic, and chances are, they'll prove you right.

I hope by now you've realized that Cinderella was as responsible for creating magic as the Fairy Godmother was. It was always a joint effort. Magic didn't happen TO Cinderella; magic happened because of her.

And one of the critical ways that Cinderella contributed to her magic was by making it easy for others to opt in to her dream.

To make any future come true, you need others to opt in to it with you. And by opting into the future with you, they're giving you some of their magic. The combination of your potential and their magic is what creates a future together.

Their magic could be as simple as money to fund the future—magic in the form of everything from a salary to investments in your project or idea.

Or their magic could be their knowledge—you might need specific skills complementary to yours to create this future you envision.

Or their magic might be their relationships—maybe you need someone to introduce you to someone new.

I've said this before, but I can't emphasize it enough. When you make it easy for others to recognize and remember your potential, you make it easy for them to give you some of their magic.

They won't just give their magic as a favor, either. They'll be delighted to provide you with their magic. They'll want to be part of your story.

It doesn't matter who you are or what you do. We are all part Cinderella, trying to make our dreams come true, and all part Fairy Godmother, noticing the potential in others and wanting to be part of making the magic happen.

So I leave you with two simple questions.

For the Cinderella me—how can I make it easy for others to opt in to the Future Me?

For the Fairy Godmother me—who needs my particular kind of magic?

Find out the answer to both, and you'll discover you truly can make all sorts of amazing dreams come true, just like Cinderella did.

Ready to implement this idea? I'll guide you through it.
Go to talesofpotential.com/discover

How to Keep Going

You just learned a lot of new ideas about creating a sparkling future for yourself inside a fairy tale framework. Now, it's time for you to take the ideas out into the real world.

Don't worry if you don't know what that looks like or how to do it. I've got you covered in the *Tales of Potential Discovery Experiments* at talesofpotential.com/discover.

Each Discovery Experiment includes:

Idea—a short video explaining how modern leaders might think about this idea in the real world.

Experiment—an easy-to-complete experiment to show the idea's immediate impact.

Amplify—questions and suggestions on how to amplify the concept.

Invest — if you're intrigued, learn how to invite us to implement this idea in your team or organization.

I've had the opportunity to watch teams transform how they collaborate and create the future with each other using many of these ideas. They're the first step in deploying Opt-In strategies in your workplace.

I hope to see you on the site—because I believe that everyone's dreams come true when we're opting in to a future with each other.

Acknowledgments

"Ambitions never manifest alone."

My list is long. It's long because people inspire me at every turn. I've been lucky to have many people challenge me and suggest I could be more.

So, Abe Castro, Adam Power, Adam Shor, Alexis Fosler, Alison Rusk, Allan Bates, Allan Milham, Amanda Morgan McAllister, Amber Allen, Andrea Byrn, Anju Ahuja, Annie Rogaski, Anthony Carrick, Azra Mehdi, Bill Vogel, Brad Justus, Blair Coffman, Bob Hebdon, Brad Serwin, Bruce Jahnke, Bruno Giussani, Bryony Wells, Candace Rypisi, Cara Marriott, Cary Tilds, Caroline Bremner, Caroline Hutt, Cecilia Spoor, Charlotte Meyer, Chelsea Paliano, Chris Paliani, Chris Record, Chris Rogaski, Christine Kenna, Christy Foley, Cindy Barry, Claribelle Van Holland, Colleen LaFontaine, Cristina Mancini Jones, Dana Blakenship, Darby Heston, Darcie DeLashmutt, Dave Smith, Dayna Shaw, Deb Roth, Debbie Frank, Delida

Costin, Dennis Coleman, Drew Sechrist, Dyna Boen, Elena Elkina, Elisa Camahort Page, Ellen Snee, Emerald Archer, Emily Della Maggiora, Emily McLanahan, Eric Mathewson, Erica Gragg, Erica Kuhl, Erik Panu, Erin Rand, Ezra Kucharz, Evon Reeves, Freddy Bunkers, Grant Parr, Gus Bates, Guy Raz, Harriet Bates, Harry Heston, Hayley Werner, Heidi Browing, Inna Effress, Jaime (Shirley) Shearls, James Smith, Jane Huxley, Janine Stein, Jennifer Bunkers, Jennifer Hungerbuhler, Jenny Lee, Jerry Gately, Jessica Shor, Jessica Steel, Jessie Vietz, Jill Siff, Jill Orr, Jim Walter, JL Pomeroy, Joan Heath, Joan Fallon, Joan Thompson, Joanna Fassl, Jonathan Sol, Joe Kennedy, Joe Griffard, John Stewart, John Trimble, Jory Des Jardins, Josh Lax, Julie Davenport, Julie Kirby, Karen Royer, Kate Shortley, Katie Davies, Kelley Kessler, Kelly Novak, Kelton Rhoads, Kerrie Mohr, Kexin Chen, Kim Kenny, Kim Le, Knox Pitzer, Kylie Kim, Laura Froelich, Lauriann Serra, Laurie Weisberg, Lavonna Jahnke, Lelani Latimer, Leslie DeHoff, Linda Baddour, Lisa Edwards, Lisa Gilliam, Lisa Serwin, Lisa Suennen, Lisa Teele, Lizzi Hamer, Lori Bonn Gallagher, Lori McLeese, Lorraine Fox, Lorraine Hendrickson, Louisa Shipnuk, Lucy Heston, Mai Green, Machelle Vietz, Mandy Cole, Marc Friedman, Maria Sipka, Maria Fernandez Guajardo, Marjorie Goux, Mark Castrovinshi, Matt Heston, Matt Morgan, Mel Brown, Merriman Mathewson, Michael Schell, Mickey Wilson, Mitch Musgrove, Mona Sabet, Morra Aarons-Mele, Nansy Bloor, Neil Mix, Nick Stewart, Nicole Parr, Nicole Reber, Paul LaFontaine, Peter Bloor, Peter Laughter, Phil Kearney, Rachel Tubman, Raisa Effress, Rafi Baddour, Randy Cohen, Rebecca Blakenship, Rebecca Zucker, Ried Elenich, Rob Barron, Rob Beeler, Robert Bellah, Robin Wolaner, Rosabel

Tao, Rose Steinberg, Rumi Tsuchihashi, Sally Drexler, Sarah Carlisle, Sarah Lacey, Sarah Shewey, Sarah Wagner Rayburn, Sarita Jha, Seema Bhatt, Shannon Nash, Shelby Scarbrough, Shenan Reed, Simone Fong, Sophie Bates, Stacey DeLarios, Stephanie Lone, Stephanie Eidelman, Steve Cakebread, Steve Sullivan, Sue Bunnell, Sue Fennessy, Sue Siegel, Suzie Reider, Taly Yaniv, Temperance Claire Huffstetter, Teryle Aguilar, Theresa Kushner, Thomas Bates, Tim Freccia, Tim Westergren, Tom Jones, Tom Shields, Tracey Solanas, Trish Fritz, Trish Gregovish, Una Fox, Wendy McEwan, Whitney Hayes, Yolanda Harris, Yvette Smith

I have stories about each of you - stories where you were my Fairy Godmother (or Fairy Godfather), stories where you've helped me see my potential.

Thank you all for nudging me toward my ambitions.

A special shout-out goes to the team of people who made this book a dream come true.

To Kelly, Simone, Yolanda, Ried, Jessie, Kylie, and Karen—thanks for patiently smiling and nodding every time I said, "I need to write a book." And for making everything else happen while I did.

To Annie—for listening to me for hours as I wrote and rewrote these pages in my head long before I put pen to paper.

To Raisa—your illustrations brought life to this book.

To Robin and Lisa—thanks for your wise counsel.

To Rumi—thank you for finding my voice with me.

To Cristina—thanks for reminding ME I'm not awesome by accident and betting on me at every turn. Your potential is my potential, and my potential is yours.

And to Randall Reeves, my Prince Charming. We're still figuring out our "Happily Ever After," and I wouldn't want to write that fairy tale with anyone else.

About the Author

JOANNA BLOOR,
CAREER FUTURIST & AMBITION GUIDE

What do you want people to opt in to? I've asked nearly 2,000 people that simple question since starting this work in 2015. The answers have led to shifting perspectives, building confidence, and transforming how people think about themselves.

In our work, we're either bored, stuck, scared, OR opting in. The choice of which one you want your team to optimize for seems obvious, right?

I have 25 years of experience helping ideas come to life. I built my career on creating futures that didn't exist before—from early Web 1.0 with Ticketmaster and Cars.com to Web 2.0 and Pandora. In each situation, we had to balance the needs of today with where we thought the industry could go. Agility and speed were always must haves while thinking towards a preferable future that made ideas into legacies. I was an Ambition Guide for these brilliant ideas.

In 2015, I turned my attention to the most exciting product in a company—people. We engage with new technologies because we recognize their potential to provide value to us in the future. I asked myself, isn't the same true for people? And isn't potential the human product that never existed before? So why aren't we using the same lessons learned to help people build their careers and confidently navigate this new future of work?

As a Career Futurist, I see the same opportunity for transformation in the world of work.

When you work on the edges of technology, you have to think like a Futurist—exploring the possible, probable, plausible, and preferable futures. You have to re-imagine frameworks and systems that don't exist.

We've seen companies transform industries—Google, Airbnb, Uber, PayPal, Amazon—the list continues. In each case, they've questioned and re-imagined a new framework for their business.

Why then, I ask, are we still using the tools, data, systems, and strategies anchored in the language and frameworks of the industrial past? Isn't it time to explore the tools of talent and build frameworks that recognize their skills, personality, and potential?

||||||||||||||||||||||||||||||||||||||||||||||||||||||||||||||||||||

Made in the USA
Monee, IL
19 October 2024

68205708R00105